ALL EXCEPT THE BASTARD

Alan Coren's contributions to *Punch* and
the *Evening Standard*, his bestselling
IDI AMIN books and his many humour
collections, including the recent highly
successful GOLFING FOR CATS and
THE SANITY INSPECTOR, have established
him as one of the funniest writers in
Britain today.

'A comic genius'   *The Times*

'Constantly funny, constantly true'
                                              Evening Standard

'Alan Coren's satirical pieces are the real thing:
fresh, sharp and coloured with a personal
fantasy'   *Daily Telegraph*

'A very topical comedian ... unusually
versatile'   *Observer*

'One of our most consistent and prolific
funny writers'   *Yorkshire Post*

**Also by the same author,
and available in Coronet Books:**

The Dog It Was That Died
The Sanity Inspector
Golfing For Cats

All Except the Bastard

Alan Coren

CORONET BOOKS
Hodder and Stoughton

FOR MARTHA AND SAM

© 1969, 1976 Alan Coren

First published in Great Britain 1976
by Robson Books Ltd.

The author wishes to express his thanks to the Editor
and Proprietors of *Punch* for permission to reproduce
material which originally appeared in its pages.

Coronet edition 1978

Printed and bound in Great Britain for
Hodder and Stoughton Paperbacks, a
division of Hodder and Stoughton Ltd.,
Mill Road, Dunton Green, Sevenoaks,
Kent (Editorial Office: 47 Bedford
Square, London, WC1 3DP) by
Hunt Barnard Printing Ltd.,
Aylesbury, Bucks.

ISBN 0 340 22339 1

Contents

THE CHRONICLES OF MAGOON

*Today London,
Tomorrow the World!*

'The first thing we have to do,' said the President of Magoon, 'is get me a crown. And some ceremonial boots.'

'An orb,' said the Minister of Transport. 'An orb would be nice. Add a bit of class.'

'And sceptres,' said the Postmaster General. He tugged his goatskin discreetly over his left nipple. 'We could all have sceptres. The whole Cabinet. With them gold knobs on the end.'

'Luminous,' said the Foreign Secretary. 'So's they'd know who we were in the dark.'

'And the pictures,' said the P.M.G. 'They'd know who we were in the pictures. We wouldn't have any nonsense then about telling the people in front to shut their rotten faces because some of us have come here to see the film. We'd just wave our sceptres about a bit. That'd keep 'em quiet.'

'And if they didn't belt up then,' said the Home Secretary. 'We'd have 'em down the Home Office and on the thumbscrews before you could say Jack Robinson.'

The Cabinet applauded vigorously. It was such fun being Independent. They'd been Independent all morning, and it had been the finest morning any of them could remember. They'd decorated the Parliamentary hut with bunting filched from the departing Royal Navy frigate (the message, stretched across the Speaker's rostrum, read: STUFF YOU, PALMERSTON), laid on jam teas for the thirty-five new M.P.s, and their families, declared war on an uninhabited hippo sanctuary in the Magoon Estuary, sent an ambassador off to Washington on the afternoon bus, declared an Englishman who arrived to cover the celebrations for *Woman's Own* persona non grata and eaten him, and they were now holed up in the Ministry of Pensions with a crate of bamboo wine and an exercise book in which they were going to draft the Constitution.

'Tell you what,' said the Minister of Defence suddenly. His eyes shone like glacé cherries beneath the rim of his tin helmet, and his mouth trembled with excitement. 'We could get a King!'

They looked at him.

'A *King*?' whispered the Minister of Agriculture and Fisheries.

'Yes. You know, a tall bloke, with an inbred conk and a bit of dignity. We could teach him to eat off a plate, and get him a throne and a pair of shoes, the lot.'

The silence would have been longer had it not, at that moment, been shattered, along with the hut's one window, by a rock, which landed at the President's feet. He picked it up, and unfolded a note which had been wrapped around it.

'It's from the Leader of the Opposition,' he said.

'We haven't got an Opposition,' said the P.M.G.

'We have now,' said the President. He cleared his throat, and read: 'You've had your whack at running the country, so clear off and let someone else have a go. Unless you're out of the Parliamentary hut by sundown, me and the Shadow Cabinet'll be up there and fill the lot of you in. Yours faithfully, Mbo Nga, Leader of the Opposition.'

The Home Secretary blew his nose on a corner of the mat.

'They don't give you a bloody chance, do they?' he said. 'Here we are, we've been fighting for Independence for thirteen effing years, we lead the people out of the wilderness, and first thing you know everyone wants to set the dogs on you.'

'Where did you go wrong?' asked the Minister of Transport.

'Don't ask me,' said the President gloomily. 'We took our lead from London. Like everyone else, when they go Independent. Says so in the manual. Follow the pattern, it says. Seven hundred and fifty years of democracy. Keep one eye on Westminster and you can't go wrong. Look at Ghana, mate – going like a bomb. Or Australia. Or Zambia.'

' 'Course,' said the Foreign Secretary reflectively, 'they had a different lot to model on, didn't they? *They* had Conservatives.'

'Shouldn't make no odds,' said the P.M.G. 'All democracy, isn't it?'

'We've only been in five hours,' said the Minister for Economic Affairs. 'What do they expect? You can't stabilise the coconut in five hours. Takes time. You got things to take into consideration. Like the Swiss franc. Like the Deutschmark.'

'Got all them gnomes in Tanzania,' said the President. 'They're on the go all day and half the bloody night, trying to discredit the coconut in the world's markets.'

'It's not difficult,' muttered the President. 'There can't be many countries in the world with a balance of payments crisis by the population eating the currency.'

'That's their whole trouble,' said the Home Secretary. 'Load of unsophisticated twits, our population. Can't see further than the ends of their hooters. Don't understand long-term planning, centralised control, regularised wages and incomes.'

The Minister of Defence drained his gourd and burped sadly.

'In the old days,' he murmured, 'we could've had that King I was talking about. We could've all had long white trousers and bent swords and teapots. Bridge in the afternoons, maids, top hats, everything. We could've had a baboon season, with hunt balls and all that caper. Debutantes and polo and *The Illustrated Magoon News* and the Gay Gordons and baccarat. Look at India. We left it too late, that's all.'

'Instead of which, we kicked off this morning with a Corporations Tax and Nationalisation of the Raffia Industry,' said the Minister of Transport.

'A right cock-up that Corporations Tax was as well,' said the P.M.G. 'We only had one Corporation, Nkoko's Inflatable Beds, and when he heard the news he packed

9

the whole lot up in a suitcase and emigrated. As for the Raffia Industry, it refuses to be nationalised, and I don't see what we can do about it. Unless we apologise, they'll hop it as well.'

Gloom fell across the pondering moot. A few hours before, it had all seemed so bright, so fine, so full of promise and hope. It was terrifying, now, thinking of the Opposition up on the hill, drafting its manifesto and honing its spears. As the shadows lengthened, a low cry filtered into earshot.

'Eeningstannard,' cried the voice, 'Alleresults!'

The Home Secretary left the hut, and returned with the newspaper. His step was light, and they looked up eagerly.

'Look!' he cried. 'Magoon's first national daily! A free press, essential to the workings of a true social democracy!'

The President grabbed the paper and spread it out on the ground in front of him. The others craned. For several seconds they crouched there in the failing light, staring, not moving, over the corpse of their dream. A sob was choked back, a gasp was stifled, and a communa shudder ran through the Cabinet.

'COME OFF IT, NBOBO!' screamed the headline, in two-inch capitals. Below it, in slightly smaller type, was a heading which ran: 'The First Five Hours.' The whole of the front page, with the exception of a rough woodcut depicting the President being roasted on a spit, was given over to an account of the Government's utter failure to develop a nuclear deterrent, join NATO, annex Rhodesia, stamp out swine fever, raise the birth-rate, force the devaluation of the dollar in terms of the coconut, put a Magoonian into orbit around the Moon, create a motor industry, build four hundred thousand mud huts, discover oil and abolish income-tax.

The President turned, with a shaking hand, to the news pages.

'The unions have called a General Strike,' he croaked.

'What unions?' said the Minister of Labour.

'They must have formed while we were having tea,' said the President. 'They've dug a bloody great hole and buried the Civil Service in it. And the Yampickers Union has eaten the whole of last month's output as a demonstration of solidarity.'

'But that's our export industry,' cried the Foreign Secretary.

'They refuse to pick another yam,' said the President, until we reinstate the schizophrenic who burned the packing-plant down last week, and put redundant workers on time-and-a-half. They want a dartboard as well.'

The Minister of Defence held a fragment of stop press up to the light, and stuffed a fist into his mouth. The Minister for Education snatched it from him.

'The aircraft workers are rioting,' he whispered.

'But we haven't got an aircraft industry.'

'That's why they're rioting. Their union claims that our failure to create an aircraft industry is forcing thousands of potentially skilled workers into menial and degrading jobs.'

'Hallo,' said the P.M.G., 'the Army's revolted and taken the rifle with it.'

'That rifle's loaded,' said the Minister of Defence somberly. He put his tin helmet back on. The others looked at it greedily; but if they had any plans to do more than that, they were not to be given the opportunity. As the last sliver of sun dropped below the swampy horizon, the bamboo door burst open, and framed in the murky gap stood the Leader of the Opposition with his Cabinet Ministers marshalled at his back. They were all wearing Harris Tweed plus-fours and check caps and Old Etonian ties around their waists. And in their hands they carried meat cleavers, which glinted dully in the twilight.

The Home Secretary plucked feebly at his President's sleeve.

'What is it?' he croaked, 'What is it?'

The President took a bicycle chain from under his loin-cloth, wrapped it around his right fist, and sighed.

'It's a General Election,' he said.

The New Immorality

Across the tiny, fetid expanse of Magoon, latest of Africa's independent republics, the monsoon gouted down, green and gloomy. The six thousand inhabitants, to avoid going mad from the incessant plopping of raindrops on the mbona leaves, had all retired to their holes to watch *Batman,* and the only movement on the surface of the saturated territory was the sluggish drift of a dugout punt, circling aimlessly on the ornamental lake in front of the Houses of Parliament. Or, more accurately, in front of where the Houses of Parliament had stood until the day before, when the Loyal Magoon Opposition had kicked them down in a fit of pique.

In consequence, the punt was now the pro tem home of the Magoon Cabinet: they sat, wretched, with the oily rain streaming down their Gannex macs (an Independence gift from London), pondering the latest stumbling-block to Magoon's chances at the top tables of the world. Due to its unique geographical position at the crossroads of Africa, the Gross National Product of Magoon consisted of tolls levied against neighbouring heads of state who wished to cross Magoon in order to see how other states were getting on, either to subvert them, or to offer them their professional services. This also meant that a national defence system was unnecessary, since everyone needed Magoon as a buffer state, and could not take the risk of occupying it.

Yet, while Magoon seemed to enjoy a Utopian situation, wooed by everyone, coveted by no one, and self-sufficient without the irritation of having to produce anything, all was not well. As the P.M. was constantly telling his flock, economic sufficiency was not enough: as a lifelong fan of *Readers Digest* and anything else he could pinch, he entertained shimmering visions of transforming Magoon into a torch of tolerance and progressive thought by whose glow the whole world might be illuminated. He saw himself as the Father Of His People, a truth which seventy per cent of the female population stood ready to endorse, and had done much to introduce such enlightened legislation as the Cabinet Ministers' Droit de Seigneur Act (1966) and the Official Ordinance maintaining the Divine Right of Prime Ministers in perpetua.

But still the age-old rigid moral structure of Magoon stood in his way: until the people could be persuaded to relax the moral code that made them a laughing-stock throughout the civilised world, Magoon's dream of becoming the pilot of the world's enlightenment would remain just that. It was to this end that the P.M. had convened the extraordinary Cabinet meeting that currently stared gloomily from the gunwales of the punt at the pitted surface of the lake.

'Bleeding cesspool of Victorian puritanism,' said the P.M. at last, 'that's what we are. A Mockery of Freethinking. I was reading in *The Times* where even the British Church refuses to condemn extramarital sexual intercourse out of hand. And look at us!'

The Cabinet stared at him from their sodden cushions. As the P.M. was the only Magoonian allowed to read outside papers, the news left them somewhat uncertain. The Minister of Finance cleared his throat.

'What's sexual intercourse?' he said.

The P.M. looked at him bitterly.

'You're an ignorant sod, Ngaga,' he said. 'No idea what goes on outside, have you? It's gobbling.'

The Cabinet frowned, puzzled.

'They only just started gobbling in Britain, then?' asked one.

'Of course not!' snapped the P.M. 'But British society expects it to be confined to married couples.'

The punt suddenly rocked with wild laughter. Swans

13

flew up from the lake in fear, and, on the bank, the watching baboons barked.

'Pull this one,' cried the Chancellor of the Exchequer, wiping his eyes, 'it's got bells on!'

'I swear it,' said the P.M. 'They can only do it after going through some recognised form of official ceremony.'

'I never heard such a load of rubbish,' said the Minister of Transport. 'Next thing, you'll tell us they just do it to have kids.'

'More or less,' said the Prime Minister.

The Cabinet snorted, and spat, and stamped their naked feet.

'And you call *them* enlightened,' said the Chancellor.

'They're changing,' said the P.M. Then he paused, watching them. Slowly he smiled. 'In England,' he said, 'there's no such sin as eating.'

The Cabinet gasped.

'It's true,' said the P.M. 'There's no set times, no rules, no secrecy, nothing. *Men and women actually eat together –*'

'They'd see one another's mouths!' shrieked the Chief Whip.

' – even children. They don't eat alone, in cupboards, like us. They even eat *in public*! In large groups.'

'It's disgusting!' cried the Cabinet. 'It's vile!'

The P.M. leaned forward, grinning.

'They even eat because they *enjoy* it !' he whispered. 'Not just to keep alive. Not just to satisfy a biological function.'

The Cabinet sat stunned. But, after a moment or two, they began to glance at one another, tentatively. The P.M. sighed heavily.

'You don't have to look like that,' he said. 'I know what you lot get up to when the lights are out. Nice square meal in the cupboard at home, all a man could want, you still can't resist nipping round the corner for a bit of how's-your-father with the odd ham sandwich, can you? Or a nice piece of fatty wort-hog. Or a peanut.'

The Chancellor shrugged.

'It goes on,' he said. 'We're only human.'

14

'Exactly,' said the P.M. 'What I want to do is bring it all out into the open. A New Morality. Put Magoon in the forefront of civilisation, see? Let My People Eat. Have State-licensed restaurants, the lot: look how much better that'd be than having our teenagers crawling off to dark alleys for a quick yam, never knowing what they might pick up. We'd have government services helping people having trouble with their eating lives. Have clinics, too. These days, half the country has indigestion, only they're too terrified of the social stigma to go to a doctor. They can cure it now, you know. Food Without Shame, lads, that's our motto.'

They had listened, awestruck, and now, like intelligent employees the world over, they cheered their leaders to the echo, and, singing a hitherto forbidden shanty about a woman who could never get enough boiled cabbage, they struck out for the sodden shore.

During the next few weeks, controversy raged. The Opposition claimed that the Government was in the pay of the greengrocers, the Magoonian national broadsheet was filled with stories of incontinent flaming youth who'd scoffed themselves into early graves, and much was made of the Undermining Of Civilisation As We Know it. Yet open controversy is itself a kind of freedom, and before long, facts hitherto ignored or suppressed began to surface. Statistics emerged: sixty per sent of Magoonians had never really experienced true intestinal satisfaction, thirty per cent confessed to having had at least one illicit meal, twenty per cent wanted to allow communal eating between consenting adults, and half the country was prepared to compromise by eating with the lights on. Pundits appeared, and waxed rich, men who wanted eating habits taught in the schools, who wanted food shown in the cinema, who wanted eating clubs established. Tales were told of vile eating orgies in the hills, where couples swopped packets of sandwiches, of evil old Magoonians who pressed boiled sweets into little girls' hands and hung about on street-corners exposing individual pork pies. A noted Magoonian intellectual appeared on TV and shouted 'Eat off!' during a debate on the Irish Question. And, bit by inevitable bit, permissiveness extended until the people thought about

15

nothing but food and whether they were getting as much of it as the next man and if they were really enjoying it at all and if too much of it made your hair fall out. Books appeared with titles like *Eating Problems At 45* and *Is Heavy Chewing A Sin?* and soon everyone was more worried about food and the eating of it than they had ever been before. Magazines sprang up, with glossy gatefolds of cod and chips and columns of advice to those without teeth, and Magoon was suddenly filled with seedy frankfurter joints and egg clubs. And lust piled upon lust, and neurosis upon neurosis, and doubt upon doubt, until, very, very late in the day, the Church of Magoon at last came out with its definitive statement:

THE GREAT TOAD SAYS EATING'S ALL RIGHT

But by then nobody had any appetite left at all.

Arms and the Men

The Prime Minister of Magoon (newest, you will remember, of the new Independencies) had had a rough morning. Even the normal vicissitudes of office had been somewhat more trying than usual: word filtering across the border from Sierra Leone had tempted his wife's brother, after an apolitical lapse of three weeks, to seize the radio station yet again and set himself up as Emperor. The now ex-Prime Minister had been halfway through his Shreddies when the brother-in-law, after a couple of shots and a dwindling shriek, had broken into *Housewives' Choice* to announce the coup. Gloomily, he had gone upstairs to pack, but before his carrier-bag was half filled a runner arrived with the news that the Emperor had gone into hiding and been replaced by a nine-man military junta (the entire army). The P.M. sighed, and paused, considering a pair of mauve socks and the unfathomable ways of Man; but hardly had the former been folded and tucked in alongside his ukelele (an Independence gift from the Warden of the Cinque Ports) when the telephone rang. The army, on discovering that the wall-safe in the Parliamentary Hut contained nothing but a packet of Weights and a copy of *The Perfumed Garden*, had deserted en masse; the junta was therefore no more, and the Acting Lance Corporal in charge, before disappearing into the bush, had sent his best respects to the ex-Prime Minister and invited him to form a new cabinet. Since the old cabinet had actually been in bed during these three constitutional upheavals and consequently had had no idea of the ups and downs of their political careers, the Prime Minister had imagined that the day's gubernatorial problems were at last settled.

Whistling, he went downstairs to finish his breakfast.

The Minister of Defence was waiting for him, eating Nescafe with a soupspoon and sighing brokenly. He looked up from beneath his tin helmet and gazed at the P.M. with tiny red-rimmed eyes.

'Something wrong, Ngogo?' said the P.M.

'You should live so long,' said the Minister of Defence. He took a rag from his battledress pocket and blew his nose erratically. 'The oil slick disappeared during the night.'

'I don't believe it,' said the P.M. He walked out onto the verandah. Beneath him, the green waters of the Awawi River rolled on taintlessly, sparkling in the morning rain. He trudged back into the shack.

'How could it happen?' he muttered.

It was a bitter blow. Five days before, Ogo Nzizi, Magoon's itinerant cutprice grocer, had been paddling upstream from his wholesaler, when his dugout sprang a leak and capsized, hurling a month's supply of groundnut oil into the Awawi. The patch, some twelve feet in diameter, had begun to drift towards the shore, occasioning much governmental rejoicing: a by-election setback (in which the pro-government candidate had been fed piecemeal to a colony of passing ants) combined with a sudden drop in productivity due to an outbreak of dancing, had left the P.M. and his cabinet feeling particularly liverish; the incident of the oil had been a golden opportunity for them to stage a lightning comeback. Launched on a wave of Churchillian oratory by the P.M., the whole glorious machinery of Magoonian government had swung into action: an interim committee had been set up to consider ways of thinking about what to do; a standing committee had been established to keep an eye on the interim committee; an Extraordinary Order In Plenary had been passed to get the National Fire Service back from his holiday; a special commission was convened with the object of composing press handouts on the steps the government was taking in setting up new committees; a Grand Pontoon Tournament had been organised by the army (this was before its political aspirations had come to a head) in aid of Distressed Committee-Members' Wives; and, as a

18

security measure, the Opposition had been put in a hole.

And now the oil had gone.

'You realise what this means?' said the Minister of Defence.

The Prime Minister nodded wretchedly. For five days, Magoon had been welded together in a non-party nationalistic fervour against the common enemy. Sixty per cent of the population were actually serving on committees of one kind or another, and the other forty per cent were making sandwiches for them and cheering. More important, the newspaper had given itself over entirely to pictures and poems and crossword competitions about the oil, while all the time one of the grimmest national scandals ever to threaten Magoon had been brewing and fermenting newslessly; now, suddenly, its ugly head was bound to be raised above the vanished oil.

'If only we'd had two more days,' said the P.M.

'We could've had Nbristil and Msidli out of the country by Tuesday,' said the Defence Minister. 'What now?'

'We'll have to have them over for tea,' said the PM. 'Maybe they've thought of something. They're good at that.'

If a touch of sarcasm had edged his voice, it was only natural. Nbristil and Msidli, whose family had been turning out clubs, and arrowheads, and curare, and hand-axes for generations of Magoonian warriors, had, on Independence, given the official government contract to manufacture arms exclusively; there had been one or two rival firms, it is true, but due to the inadequacy of their assorted products, none of their executive boards had survived the preliminary discussions with Nbristil and Msidli, who had waylaid them on the path to the Ministry of Defence, and disembowelled them to a man. A contract had been drawn up for twelve sticks, pointed, Magoon Light Infantry for the use of, at an agreed price of eighteen shillings the lot: Nbristil, who was the financial brains, was to collect the sticks, and Msidli, the technical genius, was responsible for sharpening them.

Costs, however, had rocketed. In order to have a negotiating machinery between Nbristil and Msidli on the one hand, and the Ministry of Defence on the other, it had

19

been necessary to set up a Civil Service. The man appointed had been given the job on the strength of his ability to read, but his knowledge of weapons was limited; he had had to recruit two warriors, at considerable expense, to judge the merits of the Nbristil-Msidli pointed sticks. These two warriors, being somewhat slow on the uptake, had agreed, on being approached by Nbristil, that eighteen bob was a ridiculously low figure, in view of the sudden changes in Magoon's economic position and the unexpected uncertainty of the coconut in terms of sterling in the world's markets, and had reported this to the Civil Service, who, knowing nothing about weapons himself and being currently engaged on inventing a postage stamp and traffic lights, immediately acquiesced.

At the end of six months, three pointed sticks were delivered to the Ministry of Defence with a bill for fourteen million pounds.

The press, in the shape of the Magoon Daily Advertiser, had been about to leap on this gross mismanagement of public funds when the oil slick story broke; and since the paper possessed only one typewriter, the arms scandal passed unnoticed, and would have blown over completely had the oil not decided to do so first.

'Is that Mboto Nbristil?' shouted the P.M. into the telephone. 'I was wondering if you and Msidli would come over here for a cup of tea and a natter? I'm afraid we're going to have to settle this cock-up after all. The oil's disappeared.'

He put the phone down, and the Minister of Defence went to put the kettle on. Within five minutes the Rolls-Royce of Nbristil and Msidli murmured up to their front door, pursued by a crowd of shrieking children; it was the only motor-car in Magoon. The two armaments men climbed down, immaculate in pinstripe loincloths and black homburgs with human ears tucked in the gleaming brims. The P.M. bowed them inside.

'We admit,' said Msidli, biting into a chocolate wholemeal thoughtfully, 'that a certain discrepancy may be said to exist between the original commission quotation of eighteen bob and the final delivery price of fourteen million pounds. However,' and here he grinned cannily at the PM, 'we are certain you would agree that to draw attention to this would be to discredit both your government and the Civil Service for not having had the sense – if you will pardon the expression – to cost your defence estimates adequately.'

'Therefore,' said Nbristil, 'Msidli and I are prepared to compromise in order to save the good name of Magoon and her illustrious leaders. We have agreed . . . '

'Graciously agreed,' said Msidli.

' . . . graciously agreed to return what we have told the press is, in our consideration, an unreasonable profit, in view of Magoon's present economic difficulties. That way, we come out as generous patriots, and you come out as the sort of leader who can charm the fleas out of a hedge-hog.'

The P.M. beamed.

'What sort of figure did you have in mind?' he said.

Nbristil and Msidli bent over their abacuses and went to work with their pencils. After about twenty minutes, they looked up.

'We'll let you have eleven and fourpence,' they said.

The whole thing worked out splendidly. Nbristil and Msidli received knighthoods and bronze statues, the Prime Minister was hailed as the saviour of his people by the Magoon Daily Advertiser, and the army returned from the jungle under a general amnesty to take delivery of its new pointed sticks. Naturally, there had to be a scapegoat, and since the Civil Service had clearly cost the taxpayers £13,999,999 8s. 8d., he was hung in a gaa-gaa tree and ignited.

Naturally enough, there were some dissident murmurs about a Defence Ministry that couldn't pick a decent Civil Service, but to allay these accusations and generally shore up his other domestic difficulties, the Prime Minister immediately decided on a foreign diversion, and declared war on Kapapwi.

The new pointed sticks proved a pretty poor match for Kapapwi's Starfighters; but it was generally agreed that Magoon's magnificent soldiers had borne themselves with honour. Nbristil and Msidli sent the best wreath that money could buy.

A Question of Priorities

The monsoons could not have hit Magoon (newest, you will remember, of the new independencies) at a worse time. Had it been spring, with fresh sweet showers blowing off the shimmering Awawi River, with the wingless gau-gau birds scurrying about frantically in their endearing lust, with the coruscating purple fuchsia sprouting in every living-room wall, then the drear hell of Magoon's economic problems would have been endurable. The Government would have organised a high jump contest, and a jam tea, and a nationwide marathon foxtrot, and a hippo barbecue (the way they always did at times of distress and political disorder), and the population would have smiled and sang and made love, and ignored such national sores as the devaluation of the coconut and the fiasco of the incomes policy.

But as it was, the rain came down, gouts of warm gloom, and moated them in with misery. The population, due to the Governments housing policy, had been forced to flee the council flats that had sunk into the swamp on the first day of the rains and were currently living in the tin storage tanks sold to Magoon by an itinerant pedlar claiming to represent Esso. The man, who had promised to return the following week to drill for the oil on which he said the whole of Magoon floated, was never seen again. In consequence, they huddled in the great silver cylinders playing three-card brag and going slowly mad at the incessant drumming on the lids.

The Cabinet, of course, remained in the Parliamentary Hut, roofless though it now was, partly from loyalty, partly from a sense of national emergency, but mainly because the Opposition had taken up positions under a tarpaulin across the road, poised to move in at the first hint of Government evacuation. So the Cabinet sat, sopping, beneath the striped umbrellas which had been an Independence gift from the Duke of Gloucester (along with an annual High Jump Cup in E.P.N.S. and a lithograph of Sandringham), and pondered their national destiny.

'If only we'd played our cards right,' muttered the Foreign Secretary, 'we could've been in the Common Market by now.'

'I wrote to him, din't I?' shouted the Chancellor of the Exchequer. 'In French, and everything. Told him the Treaty of Rome was all right by us, and asked him to put the Danish bacon on the next plane out. Not a word.'

'Snubbed,' said the Prime Minister lugubriously. 'I'd take it to the U.N. if we had the fare-money.'

'We could've had Flowers Keg, knackwurst, pommes frites,' moaned the Foreign Secretary, rocking sadly on his dripping haunches, 'Frank Cooper's Oxford Marmalade, and them open sandwiches covered in prawns.'

'My brother-in-law saw this film in Lagos,' said the Minister of Transport, 'with all these Parisian bints doing the watusi in their vests. Mind you, I'm not saying it's everybody's taste.'

'It's being six thousand miles away that's done it,' said the P.M. 'We should've declared our independence somewhere sensible, like Belgium. Close to the centre of things. I could've had an Alfa-Romeo, midnight blue, bucket seats, foglight.'

'Didn't have much luck with the Russians either,' said the Foreign Secretary. 'Went to all that trouble getting ourselves overthrown by popular revolution, forking out all them coconuts on red flags and copies of *Das Kapital* and everything, all we got was a Gestetnered letter from Kosygin asking us how many Ilyushin bombers we were prepared to buy.'

'No worse than the British,' said the Chancellor. 'All we got for our request to rejoin the Empire was a tin of biscuits with a picture of a Beefeater on the lid and a ten-bob credit note for Selfridge's.'

'Cocked up the incomes policy too, didn't we?' said the Minister of Education. 'We should never have rubbed the Ground-nut Workers Union up the wrong way. They've eaten the whole of our Gross National Product for 1967 in protest.'

The Prime Minister put down his umbrella and wrung his hands.

'What's to become of us, lads?' he cried. 'Where has it gone, the glory and the dream?'

'*Eheu fugaces!*' keened the Chief Whip, who had spent his summer holidays on a tour of Balliol and the Potteries. '*Mehr licht!*'

There was a long drear pause, punctuated by the fat plopping of the rain and the jeers of the Opposition across the road. It was the Minister of Defence who shook them finally from their reveries of hemlock.

'Here!' he cried suddenly, with such force that his tin helmet flew down over his black eye-patch. 'Why don't we make a bomb?'

The Cabinet peered through the monsoon, uncertainly.

'Something nuclear,' said the Minister of Defence. 'Something with a bit of class.'

'Ngaga's got a point,' said the P.M. 'Look how they're taking the Chinese seriously all of a sudden. No more jokes about a long line of Chinamen holding hands and touching the moon.'

'No more cracks about them all standing on the Isle of Wight,' said the Chief Whip.

'Nothing about the trams going sideways,' said the Chancellor.

'Gets you respect, does a bomb,' said the Minister of Defence. 'Gets you a seat at the top tables. I can see us now, in Paris . . .'

' . . . walking up the steps of the Elysee Palace . . .'

' . . . pushing a wheelbarrow across Red Square . . .'

' . . . knocking up the White House at four in the morning . . .'

'What's that you got there?' says Nixon. 'It's a bomb' we say. 'Come in' he says, 'I'll put the kettle on.'

'Fabulous!' cried the P.M. 'We can't stop we'll say, 'we just came by about the ten billion dollar loan' 'Will a cheque do?' he says 'or would you rather have it in Cadillacs?'

The Cabinet fell deliriously silent, toying with dreams of loot and might. After a bit, the Prime Minister shook himself free.

'How do we go about making one?' he said.

The Cabinet peered at one another through the downpour.

'Well,' said the Minister of Defence, since it seemed to fall within his minuscule province, 'it's all a question of chemistry, isn't it?'

A debate ensued, with the customary heat of such things, as to where physics left off and chemistry began, but it quickly petered out in a trickle of biological anecdotes, and plans were laid to import the prerequisites of thermonuclear overkill by the next runner. Within three days (during which time the Opposition had twice crossed what was now the stream separating them from office with the object of forcing a general election at stickpoint, but had been thwarted by the weather), a parcel arrived from Hamley's containing a Lott's Junior Chemistry Set, a plastic microscope, and a book of indoor firework recipes.

'It's just a matter of native wit and a bit of luck,' said the Defence Minister, as much to conceal his disappointment as anything else. 'A bit of this, a dash of that, trial and error. That's all the Chinese had, lads.'

'Seven hundred million of them,' said the P.M. dispiritedly. 'It's like monkeys coming up with *Hamlet*. Start off with seven hundred million chemistry sets at breakfast time, you'll have a fair old nuclear stockpile by sundown.'

'Not to worry,' said the Defence Minister. 'There's a full set of instructions. They split the syllables up as well.'

They pooled their umbrellas to provide a relatively dry laboratory, and, while the Chief Whip stood guard with his blowpipe against the possibilities of coups from the forests, they set about the construction of their nuclear club card. After a day of considerable minor injury, the incineration of the Upper Chamber, and the reduction to hairlessness of two Junior Ministers, the Cabinet had constructed an orange-boxful of contents whose object was to justify the

25

legend 'A-BOM Mk.1' painted on its lid. A fuse of paraffin-soaked pipe-cleaners trailed ominously through a knot-hole. The Cabinet examined their creation ecstatically.

' 'Course,' said the Defence Minister, 'there's probably a few bugs to be ironed out. But a bomb's a bomb for a' that.'

'Pity we can't test it,' said the P.M.

'You need an atoll for that,' said the Foreign Secretary. 'Or, at the very least, a desert of some description.'

'We could test its delivery potential, though,' said the P.M. Without actually setting it off. Marvellous propaganda, if nothing else. We ought to have a dry run.'

'Is the missile back from his lunch?'

'I'll go and see,' said the Minister of Transport.

Within five minutes he was back, leading a sopping but wiry local inhabitant.

'Mbobo Ntosa,' said the M. of T. 'Fastest eight-hundred-metre man in Magoon.'

Everyone shook hands with the missile. The P.M. cleared his throat.

'What we want you to do, Mbobo,' he said. 'Is heave this atom bomb up on your shoulder, and run like the clappers. When you get to the mangrove swamp, put it down. That's all.'

'What's it worth?' said the missile.

The Cabinet murmured among itself.

'How'd an M.B.E. suit you?' said the P.M.

'Done!' said the missile, and took off towards the forest at full pelt, with the bomb bouncing on his back. The Cabinet peered towards the point where the monsoon had folded him in. He hadn't been gone more than ten seconds when there was a blinding yellow flash, a green roman candle, and an apparently disembodied catherine wheel hurtling about in the fetid gloom. After a couple of seconds, two rockets shot skywards, and the bomb went out with a disheartening hiss.

The Opposition brought back what was left of the missile, gleefully, and, leaving him to moan horribly on the step, they went back across the road to table a censure motion. The Cabinet stared down at the remains.

'Pity we haven't got a hospital,' said the Minister of Health.

'Pity we haven't got a school,' said the Minister of Education, who never passed up a cue like that.

The Prime Minister turned on them savagely.

'I wish you two would shut up about schools and hospitals!' he shrieked. 'Where do you think I'm going to get the loot for things like that? Can't you see I'm trying to build up a civilised modern state, something with a bit of authority in the world?' He walked back slowly to the littered laboratory, biting a fingernail. 'The way I see it,' he said, 'first thing tomorrow morning, we'll buy ourselves a bigger chemistry set.'

The Man with a Golden Tooth

Across the unimpressive acreage of Magoon (until a week before the newest of the new independencies), the inevitable gloom came down with the inevitable rains; the people were sodden in spirit. Not even the emergence of Mauritius as a free state had been able to lighten their darkness: although this event had conferred a nominal seniority on the midget republic by suddenly turning it into the second youngest member of the Commonwealth, rejoicing had turned instantly to gall, wormwood and ashes (as it usually did) with the pre-Budget announcement of the abolition of telegrams. This had meant that Magoon was unable to wire congratulations to the infant newcomer, a source of shame that punctured the proud heart of every Magoonian. True, the Government had attempted to offset this humiliation by crating up the Postmaster General and despatching him personally to Mauritius with a flower and a message of cheer, but the fatalism attending his departure had proved entirely justified: eight days later, the Prime Minister received word that his P.M.G. had found a lucrative position selling matches and was applying for Mauritian citizenship; worse, the word itself was contained in an ornate Mauritian telegram, an item described by the Deputy Prime Minister as a raspberry blown in the face of every citizen of Magoon.

The Deputy Prime Minister was given to statements like that. But there was nothing that the P.M. could do about it, since the continuance in office of his Deputy was the P.M.'s only hedge against assassination: many an Opposition assegai had been honed by many a member of the Shadow Cabinet, only to be hurled aside upon the realisation that the slaying of the P.M. would bring his Deputy to the leadership of the country. Not, of course, that it was easy to imagine how much lower Magoon would sink into penury and shame, but everyone accepted without reservation that if a means existed of bringing the country into greater disrepute and debt, the Deputy Prime Minister was the man to find it. He had tendered his resignation eighteen times in the past week, but the P.M. had countered each note with a rise in salary and a new medal, and refused to let his Deputy go. Worst of all, this debilitating cycle of resignation and its refusal had caused a harrowing run on Vat 69, now the only acceptable currency between Magoon and her suspicious neighbours. The whisky had been an Independence gift from the Duke of Gloucester back in 1965, and had been laid down in the vault of the Magoon Only National Bank with pride. But the Deputy Prime Minister insisted, every time a new medal was struck for him, in exchanging it for Scotch; and the bank manager, who could see no reason why his bank's insolvency should prevent his country from bestowing on him the honours commensurate with his high office, was delighted to accept the medals, which he wore at breakfast to impress his family with the stature of its head. The drain on the country's pitiful resources was incalculable, and the drain on its pitiful morale worse, since the more drunk the Deputy Prime Minister became, the more keen he was to tender his resignation and retire to the country to drink. Indeed, the standard of debate in the Parliamentary Hut had fallen to an abysmal level, consisting as it did of three speeches of resignation per day from the Deputy P.M. (including such accusations as that the Prime Minister was in fact Adolf Hitler blacked up) and three announcements by the P.M. of a rise in salary for his Deputy, which the Opposition front bench was unable to attack for fear of the consequences of the P.M.'s resignation. There was never time for Any Other Business, and it was largely as a result of this lunatic fiscal spiral that the Government had decided on a tough Budget. This, needless to say, had been decided on without consulting the

Deputy Prime Minister, who spent the night before deliberately hiding from his colleagues in order to have an excuse for resigning on the following morning, on the grounds that he hadn't been consulted.

It was the worst Budget any of them could remember. Indeed, it was the only Budget any of them could remember, since the normal practice had been to wind up every financial year with a Grand Jumble Sale of Independence gifts, to which Magoon's neighbours were cordially invited. Since Magoon had no national productivity to speak of, the main raw material being rain, nothing except these jumble profits ever flowed into the Exchequer; true, there were considerable exports of manufactured goods, but these consisted of rafts, which, the boatbuilders having finished them, were sailed to more stable economies across the sodden swamps, together with the manufacturer and his family and/or mistress. No money ever came back.

But now they had reached the last of their Independence gifts, and had no illusions about the international viability of a box of 1965 biscuits with a painting of Windsor Castle on the lid (a gift from the Arundel Herald Extraordinary), a commemorative park bench from Transport House (much of which had vanished into the digestive tracts of Hodkinson's Grey Termites), and a plumed hat dropped by the fleeing High Commissioner after the Independence Day celebrations. Nor did it seem possible to arouse world interest in Magoon: six weeks before, they had reintroduced hanging in the hope of a cheque from Duncan Sandys, who, they were sure, must have been feeling guilty about not having promised them valid British passports upon Independence and thereby confining them to the boggy misery of Magoon. However, all they had received in reply had been a brief typewritten note reminding them that they didn't have passports. They thereupon declared their new gallows open, and began hanging one another in an effort to incense the liberal world against their brutal régime; but, instead of an immediate visit by dollar-bearing Security Council teams, all that turned up was a rope-salesman from Bulawayo and a Welsh medical student who'd been expelled from Bart's for doing heart transplants on ingenuous blood donors, and was looking for fresh fields to be conquered on.

So, prompted (as they were in all things) by the model of British constitutional government, they drafted a Budget. It had been harsh, inspired, uncompromising, adventurous, brave, brutal, and as total a failure as it is possible to have in an economy already bankrupt. A few days afterward, the Cabinet found themselves squatting wretchedly in the mossy dankness of the Central Office hut, struggling for a way out of the deeper pit into which their radical, far-sighted measures had hurled them.

'It's him I blame it on,' said the P.M. bitterly, jabbing his mace at the Chancellor of the Exchequer. 'Him and his bloody income tax!'

'Nothing wrong with introducing income tax, mate,' said the Chancellor. 'What this country needs.'

'Not at thirty bob in the pound, it doesn't,' said the P.M. 'You're supposed to start small, two bob in the pound, personal allowances, that kind of thing. It's all in your book.'

'I thought we were after something drastic,' said the Chancellor.

'Ho, yes, I should think so!' cried the Deputy P.M., who had dropped in for a drink between resignations. 'We're now the only country in the world with one hundred per cent unemployment, and everyone claiming the Government now owes him ten bob in the pound for not earning anything. And whose idea was it to bang a tax on tobacco?'

'It's an accepted method . . .'

'You realise they've all packed up smoking it? They've gone over to smoking the tips. No tax on them, is there? You can go out now and buy a packet of twenty corks, and the Government don't see a penny. And I'd have thought you'd have had more sense than to put bamboo wine up to twelve quid a bottle.'

'We haven't all got your experience,' said the Chancellor nastily.

'Ho, very clever! Didn't take much experience to see they'd all start making it out of yams, did it? They turn out a fair old jar of yam chablis down the Rat and Cockle for twopence a go these days. Mind you, I'm not saying the petrol levy wouldn't have worked . . . '

'Thank you.'

' . . . if we'd had any petrol. The only consumption is in old Ngogo Nbaba's Ronson, and he went out and bought matches as soon as he heard the news. Like the road-fund licence: fat lot of good that is when the Minister of Technology hasn't even come up with a wheel yet.'

'I'm working on it, 'n'I?' shouted the Minister. 'It takes time, a thing like that. You got to work out where the corners go.'

The P.M. beat his mace furiously on the sodden floor.

'It's no good us bickering like this, lads!' he cried. 'There nothing else for it. We'll have to sell the gold reserves.'

The Cabinet gasped. The Cabinet rocked on its haunches. The Cabinet keened.

'Not the gold reserves!'

'Not our genuine eighteen-carat presentation inkwell!'

'Not the gift of our Great White Mother Across The Foam!'

'Anything but that!' they shrieked.

The P.M. held up his hand.

'Either that, lads, or we're down the labour exchange tomorrow morning, and no two ways about it.'

They sprinted through the clattering monsoon towards the Treasury shed. It was locked. They hammered on the door.

'Funny,' said the P.M. 'The Minister for Economic Affairs is supposed to be in there. With his spear and everything.'

'Not his lunch hour, is it?' said the Chancellor.

'It's half-past four,' said the P.M.

The Cabinet looked at one another briefly. Then, with a concerted shove, the door was down, and they were through. On the ceremonial bamboo plinth reserved for the golden inkwell, a rat examined a nut.

'Hallo,' said the P.M. 'Here's a do. He must've taken it down to have it polished, or . . . '

'EENINGSTANNARD!' cried a voice from the murk.

'ALLERESULTS! ECONOMICS MINISTER EMI-
GRATES! EENINGSTANNARD!

With trembling hands, the Cabinet unfolded the newspaper and pored over it. It was not so much the headline
informing them that the Minister for Economic Affairs
had emigrated to Zurich that snatched at their eyes, but
the photograph beneath it. It showed the Minister smiling
widely, but with a smile of such gleaming proportions,
such respectable yellowness, such metallic cheer, that their
hearts were left with nothing to do but sink as one.

Next day they hanged his dentist. It didn't do much to
stabilise the economy, but with all that money invested
in the new gallows, it seemed a shame, as the Deputy P.M.
put it, to pass up a golden opportunity.

Gaudeamus Igitur,
Ils Ne Passeront Pas!

'He's still outside,' said the Minister of Education.

The Prime Minister of Magoon (tiniest of the new independencies) peered through a new crack in the Parliamentary Hut, searching the downpour. Summer had come to Magoon, bringing with it an increase of ten degrees fahrenheit in the temperature of the permanent rains, for which the Magoonians, a wisely undemanding race, were duly grateful. Indeed, so calm and unrippled had the public mood been for the past few days that the Government had been unable to sleep: born in threat and forged in dissent, they mistrusted stability to the point where suspicion had, over the years, become their only professional attribute. In fact, in an effort to galvanise opposition, they had over the past week taken to fierce and widely publicised cabinet shuffling, but such was the gentleness of the public temper that the people took the whole thing as a jolly seasonal joke; a reaction not unknown in lands far older in democracy than the tiny republic.

But this morning they had woken to a threat of such magnitude that they had begun to wish for a return to the earlier apathy. For in Magoon, as elsewhere, Student Power had lashed itself into fashionable frenzy and revolted to a man. Or, more accurately, to the man, since the midget country's entire stock of higher education lay vested in the agitated figure of Nbobo Mgung, undergraduate and scourge.

'There he is,' cried the Prime Minister, as the rain broke stride, briefly. 'He's got a new banner.'

'What's it say?' said the Foreign Secretary, putting down

34

his globe and pausing in his dream of lebensraum.

The Prime Minister squinted into the murk.

' "FREADOM NOW" ' he said. He opened the window. 'Bugger off,' he shouted, 'There's people in here trying to govern!'

The student materialised gradually, stopping inches from the window.

'I shall overcome,' he sang. 'Some day-ay-ay.'

'I should cocoa!' shouted the Prime Minister. 'Over my dead body!'

'I shall not, I shall not be moved,' sang the student. He leaned forward ominously. 'You want to watch yourself, my old mate,' he said nastily. 'You're up against World Student Solidarity, so I wun't go pushing your face in where it's not wanted. We'll have Nixon out by Tuesday week, and you're next. I'd start putting my clean underwear in a bag if I was you.'

'*Were* you,' said the Minister of Education. 'Subjunctive.'

'Ho!' said the student. 'A troublemaker. I got your number, mate, trying to teach a striking student, contrary to Subsection Nine, paragraph One. We'll have your bonce up on a spike double-quick, soon as Tariq Ali gets here. I got friends.'

The Prime Minister backed away from the window.

'Is it true what he said about Nixon?'

The Foreign Secretary picked a smashed cockroach from his mace.

'It's on the cards,' he said.

'Topple a government, can they?'

'Never can tell.'

The Prime Minister reflected.

'We'd better have him in,' he said. 'Air his grievances.'

He opened the bamboo door, and Nbobo Mgung stepped in cautiously. He put down his banner, but refused to part with his brick, preferring to cradle it in his lap as he took his place cross-legged on the sodden floor.

'Well, Nbobo,' said the P.M. pleasantly, 'I'm very happy to have the chance of getting to know you better. I'm sure we can sort the whole thing out between us. What exactly is it you're studying, by the way?'

'Knitting,' said the student.

'Knitting?'

'I'm enrolled in the Emma Bagnold School of Knitting, 'n'I?' said the student. 'Postal dept. 1a, 14 Mafeking Villas, Lewisham.'

The Foreign Secretary turned his globe slowly.

'Lewisham?' he murmured, peering close.

'S.E.13,' said the student. He jabbed a finger on the globe.

The Foreign Secretary leaned towards the P.M.'s ear.

'It's bloody near Washington all right,' he whispered.

The P.M. winced, recovered, and broadened his smile.

'Well, Nbobo,' he said, 'what exactly is the trouble?'

'I want to do a balaclava helmet, don't I?' said the student.

'I'm sorry?'

'I been doing socks for eight months. I done sixty-seven bloody socks, all told. I mean, where's the free expression, where's the ideal of a progressive education? What I want is a nice bit of Fair Isle, or a lady's cable-stitch bolero suitable for afternoon or evening wear, or a two-tone balaclava helmet. Bloody Emma Bagnold won't let me do nothing but socks. Also, there's the whole burning issue of student discipline.' He pulled a crumpled fragment of Basildon Bond from his tattered op-art loincloth. 'Listen to this: "Dear Mister Mgung, I am returning herewith your exercise for lesson eight, as your Pair Of Baby Boottees appears to have one leg and four feet. Yours Faithfully, E. Bagnold (Mrs.) P.S. Unless you begin putting stamps on your letters at earliest convenience, I shall have to consider suspending you from the course".'

'What do you want me to do?' asked the Prime Minister wearily.

'Write and tell her about the balaclava helmet,' said the student. 'Also, guarantee a rise in my annual grant to cover cost of postage and packing.'

'I'll see what I can do,' said the P.M. 'Is that all?'

'For the time being,' said the student. He grinned savagely, and left, chanting *sotto voce*.

The next day passed quietly, and the Cabinet was beginning to feel it had weathered this latest storm, when, towards nightfall, Magoon's policeman appeared at the door of the hut, craving an immediate audience. His hands were full of moist blue pulp.

'What's that?' said the Home Secretary, his brother-in-law.

'It's my helmet,' said the constable. 'Or what's left of it.'

'There's no need to cry,' said the Prime Minister.

'That was an independence gift from the Dame of Sark,' said the Foreign Secretary. 'Twelve bobsworth of helmet, or I'm no judge. What have you done to it?'

The constable glared at him bitterly.

'What have *I* done to it?' he cried. 'That's the work of your bloody student, that is. Knocked it off and trod on it. With malice aforethought.'

'Why'd he go and do a thing like that?'

'He says I'm a fascist,' said the constable. 'Me who's been an Episcopalian all his working life. Says it's a protest over Vietnam, also a reprisal against the Belgians for filling in Patrice Lumumba. Plus a blow struck for Scottish Nationalism.'

'Anything else?' said the P.M.

'He wants to discuss germ warfare and the Danzig Corridor,' said the constable. 'At a teach-in with those responsible.'

The Prime Minister sighed.

'Where is he?'

'Down behind his barricade. You can't miss it, it's an oil-drum with a picture of Regis Debray on it, and a Chinese flag. He's got some kind of large sock over his head as well, in case of tear gas, he says. What's tear gas?'

'More to the point,' said the Minister of Defence, 'What's germ warfare?'

'Maybe he's worried about the tsetse-fly,' said the P.M. 'Anyway, I expect you to go down there and find out, seeing as you're the only one left with a tin helmet. And for God's sake keep the conversation off socks.'

They didn't see the Minister of Defence for three days. When he finally came back, he had a black eye, no helmet, and a sign round his neck demanding the legalisation of LSD and the reopening of the Suez Canal. In the meantime, whitewashed signs had appeared throughout the country demanding hands off Gibraltar and free contraceptive advice for all those enrolled in full-time study. The information that the Prime Minister was a twit in the pay of Enoch Powell was appended to most of these.

'I don't like it,' said the Chief Whip. 'Soon as the Opposition finishes its poker tournament and finds out what's been going on, they'll come out in support. Thing like that could drive a tram through the whole ideal of one-party democracy.'

The Cabinet collapsed into noiseless gloom. They were still pondering on possible cures for the world's ills in order to placate Nbobo Mgung and steer his thoughts away from revolution, when a discreet tap on the door shook the Parliamentary Hut.

'Who is it?' cried the P.M.

'Chairman of the Ratepayers Association,' said a posh voice.

They opened the door to a well-scrubbed citizen in a chalk-striped suit, white collar and somewhat frayed Old Wykehamist tie, patent leather shoes, and an elderly bowler hat. It was Nbobo Mgung.

'Good morning,' he said. 'May I respectfully protest against the decision to locate a concrete lamp-post in front of one of Magoon's loveliest swamps? Does tradition mean nothing any more? Also, please repatriate all immigrants, abolish trade unions, and stop people using the state flag on tea-towels. The country is going to the dogs, by Jove! Likewise, do we not feel, gentlemen, that the ridiculously high surtax is in danger of reducing us to a race of cloth-capped vulgarians, eager for nothing but battening on the country's already overloaded welfare facilities? And while you're at it, a total revision of the university grants system is called for. Respectable citizens are sick and tired of paying for lecherous drug-addicts to sit on their long-haired backsides all day, sneering at the things that made this country great.'

He paused, and they stared at him.

'What's that you've got under your arm?' said the P.M. at last.

Nbobo Mgung shrugged nonchalantly, and unrolled a

long piece of illuminated parchment, at the bottom of which the name E. Bagnold shimmered iridescently. On the owner's lip, a small supercilious smile rippled faintly.

'Since you ask,' he said, 'I graduated an hour ago.'

'On a clear day,' said the Prime Minister, 'you can see Umtasi.'

The rheumy eyes of his Cabinet peered at him through the aqueous murk. It was, as it had always been, the rainy season; which meant, the four years of their independence having brought nothing to Magoon except booming insolvency, that the state of decay of the Parliamentary Hut had reached the point where none of the Cabinet ever left it for fear of never being able to find it again, one haphazard collection of upright bamboo poles being very like another. True, there was still some roof, made up largely of vultures whose political acumen was such that they knew a good dinner when they saw one, and that it was only a question of time. So the Cabinet huddled on the sodden wattle below, shifting only when portions of the roof flew away temporarily in search of something to keep them going until the General Election.

'There aren't any clear days,' said the Minister of Defence.

'Never have been,' said the Chancellor. 'Not in living memory.'

They all pondered.

'October 17th, 1949,' said the Prime Minister at last. 'You must have been on your holidays. It cleared up around half-past ten.'

'Sun come out?' said the Chancellor.

'No,' said the P.M. thoughtfully. 'No, it was more of a bright period, really.'

'Started coming down again at a quarter to three,' said

the Minister of Education. 'Hasn't stopped since.'

'Well, anyway,' said the P.M., wringing out his fedora (an Independence gift from the Garter King of Arms), 'what I mean is, if we *had* a clear day, you could see Umtasi.'

'But it's miles away,' said the Minister of Economic Affairs, a post which had, of course, ceased to exist some time before. 'Up behind the hills.'

'That's just it,' said the P.M. 'The hills are *in* Umtasi. But the stuff that washes down off them ends up in Magoon.'

'I'm not with you,' said the Minister of Defence. Rust had, of late, taken to seeping down from his tin helmet and impairing his hearing, and the P.M. would have ignored his imperception had it not also been reflected in the eyes of his other colleagues. He sighed heavily.

'Look,' he said, pointing.

They peered through what had once been the back benches.

'That rim of black sludge,' said the P.M., 'is Umtasi. It's been creeping towards us for God knows how long, and now it's here.' He drew a moist ball of parchment from his loincloth. 'I've had this letter from their President. They've sent a soil sample away for analysis, and it turns out it's theirs. They've declared a new *de facto* border and set up a customs post and a souvenir shop, and everything.'

The Cabinet seethed.

'You're not going to let those expansionist bastards get away with that!' shrieked the Chancellor. 'There might be oil under there!'

'There's Magoon under there, which is more to the point!' cried the Minister for Economic Affairs. 'Our motherland, mate, getting seeped over by those bleeding Umtasi barbarians. If the rain keeps up, it'll all be over by Christmas. Magoon'll be nothing but a load of illegal immigrants squatting on Umtasi silt. Stateless.'

The P.M. examined the rag of letter.

'He says it's his last territorial claim in Africa,' he said. 'They're stopping where they are from now on.'

'I should cocoa,' said the Foreign Minister. 'They couldn't stop it spreading even if they wanted to, which

41

they don't. It's Attila the Hun all over again. We'll have to take action!'

The Cabinet winced, and refused to catch one another's eyes.

'I'm not taking it to the United Nations, if that's what you mean,' said the P.M. 'All that postage.'

'We'd have to buy headed notepaper and everything,' said the Chancellor.

'Well, if you think I'm going to just sit here while our precious heritage turns into a geological joke,' said the Foreign Minister, 'you got another think coming. What about economic sanctions?'

They stared at him blankly.

'You know,' he said. 'Paralyse their economy by refusing to export anything to Umtasi until they take their country back where it belongs.'

'What's export?' asked the Chancellor. They all looked at the Foreign Secretary, who had done a postal course, once. He shrugged.

'Well, it was only a thought,' he muttered. 'You could prob'ly achieve the same effect by having troop movements along their border. Terrorise 'em with a show of strength.'

'The army's off sick,' said the Minister of Defence. 'Got his boils back. Anyway, I wouldn't jeopardise his career by sending him off on a job like that. What with a moving border and everything, he could kip down one night at the end of a nice bit of peaceful manoeuvering with his pointed stick and wake up the next morning to find he was the spearhead of an invasion. Suddenly find ourselves accused of wanton aggression, or something. Suddenly find ourselves overrun with a load of Swedes in blue helmets, eating everything.'

There was a long lugubrious silence, punctuated only by the plopping of frogs on the despatch box. Finally, the Foreign Secretary spoke.

'If,' he said, 'we've ruled out economic pressure, military intimidation, and actual war, there's only one accredited method of modern diplomacy left.'

He paused dramatically. The P.M. sighed.

'Go on, then,' he said. 'Surprise me.'

'We,' said the Foreign Secretary, 'shall nick one of their airliners.'

'What?'

'Hijack it. Right under their very hooters.' His eyes glazed. 'I can see it all. Proceeding at forty thousand feet, ground speed five hundred miles per hour, all your Jet Set sitting back scoffing out of them little trays, knocking back the duty-free cherry brandy, not a care in the world, and, suddenly, this brave officer of the National Magoon Liberation Army jumps up with his pointed stick, and swipes the lot. Forces the pilot to land in Magoon. Piece of cake.'

The Cabinet applauded vigorously. Only the Home Secretary looked sceptical.

'They've only got one Tiger Moth,' he said. 'I've seen it. They use it for joy-rides round Bingaga Airport on August Bank Holiday.'

'All the better,' said the Prime Minister. 'We'd be knocking off their entire civil fleet. Not to mention their air force. Also, it's easier hijacking a plane when you're sitting behind the pilot. You just jab your pointed stick in his ear and there you are. Who's volunteering?'

'The Home Secretary,' said the Chancellor. 'He's the only one who's seen it. The rest of us might go off and come back with a BOAC Boeing, or something, and then we wouldn't half cop out.'

They dragged the Home Secretary to the door.

'We'll get a medal struck,' promised the P.M. 'Non-contributory pension scheme, brass pocket-watch, the lot.'

'Be back here four o'clock tomorrow,' shouted the Foreign Secretary, as the hero splashed away across the bog wretchedly. 'We'll have the kettle on.'

At four the following afternoon, the Cabinet, in their best ceremonial loincloths and trilbies, sat fidgeting in the Parliamentary Hut, staring up through the roof into molten greyness.

'We could ask for some loot as well,' said the P.M., as much to kill the agonising time as anything else. 'Ransom. Get the Hut done up nice. Regency striped wallpaper, a few club chairs, a Members' lav, that kind of thing. A potted palm.'

'Where is he?' said the Chancellor. 'It's nearly half-past.'

The words were scarcely out before, as one man, the Cabinet heard above the clattering rain, the sound of an engine, high above them. It grew louder. They craned their necks. Out of the east, just below the permanent cloud-cover came a dot, unsteadily. It chugged over the Parliamentary Hut, plane-sized, and became a dot again, flying west.

'He's missed us!' shrieked the Prime Minister.

'Shut up!' cried the Foreign Secretary. 'Listen!'

The dot was coming back. The Cabinet leapt from the crouch, and flung themselves outside, waving their order papers.

'OY!' they screamed. 'Down here!'

The dot disappeared in the east.

The Cabinet trooped back.

They sat down again.

'Never thought to wonder whether he'd find Magoon,' said the P.M.

Not the sort of thing that happens, usually,' said the Foreign Secretary sullenly. 'I mean, it was a good idea in principle.'

'Yes,' said the P.M. He sighed. 'It's not all beer and skittles, being the smallest country in the world,' he said. 'Diplomatically speaking.'

JOHN BULL'S OTHER ENGLAND

The Far West

It's no accident that little is done to encourage foreign visitors to approach this island from the south-west; it is an aspect singularly lacking in prestige. Shepherd them in under the cliffs of Dover, yes; usher them up the great green carriage-drive of the Solent, certainly; and if possible, leave them bobbing on the tide for a bit, squinting at the land-mass and thanking God that the race behind the beetling crags is slow to anger. But never let them in at Land's End, where the impression they will get from the bow-rails is of an extremely thin country, no more than a couple of kilometres across at its widest, and undeniably low. Legend, in fact, has it (it has almost everything in the West Country) that an excursion was mounted as early as the third century B.C. by bored Roman mariners on a forty-eight hour pass in Brest; who, having negotiated some two hundred miles of Channel in filthy weather, suddenly saw this narrow, liver-coloured atoll off the port bow and immediately put about with a pang of bitter disillusionment it took two centuries to overcome.

By one of those coincidences with which geography is rife, Land's End is the westernmost point of the English mainland, and since earliest times it has been as a magnet to Englishmen fascinated at the prospect of there being intelligent life somewhere out there beyond the mists. Indeed, five miles inland is a geegaw called Lanyon's Quoit, knocked up some four thousand years ago by men eager to balance a seventeen foot stone slab on three six-foot uprights. It has long been fashionable to regard this as a barrow, but a likelier explanation is that it was erected so that New Stone Age citizens could get a better view out to sea, in the hope that there was something edible there. The Cornish have always been a practical race.

They are also a distinct race. One of the six Celtic nations, they share with their siblings (the Scots, the Irish, the Welsh, the Manx, and the Bretons) a deep-seated scorn for Anglo-Saxons, and are constantly rooting around for an excuse to dissociate themselves from ties imposed on them by that fickle mistress, geology. They feel their closest affiliation with the Bretons, and consider the English Channel to be a purely temporary measure; Cornishmen subscribe unanimously to the belief that Atlantis is buried beneath the Waters which separate Cherbourg from the Lizard, and only live for the day when the Channel will be dredged by the U.N. and the area in question roped off and fortified against English intruders. This belief embraces the certain knowledge that the inhabitants of Atlantis, Cornishmen all, have made the requisite adjustments to the new weather conditions, and lead an idyllic existence pottering about the sea-bed in their gills and making effigies of Joan the Wad, awaiting the Day of Liberation. There is also talk of oil-rights.

The Cornish language is the only one of the Celtic tongues which has gone to join its ancestors (Sanskrit and Latin, to mourn but two), but serious efforts are being made by secessionists to resurrect it. R. Morton Nance, a pre-war Grand Bard of Cornwall, was responsible for the remarkable play, *An Balores* (The Chough), a toothsome dramatic gobbet which compares the Cornish language to a chough which has been shot dead and has come to life again. Experts on choughs say this is a fair comparison, but lay opinions differ. Suffice it to remark that the similarities between Cornish and Welsh, and the ties of ancient blood, have been enough to cause the sandwiched inhabitants of Devon grave concern; many of them feel that the slogan 'CHOOSE OR PERISH!' which has been daubed by infiltrators on walls from Plymouth to Ilfracombe constitutes a grave threat to the Devon tourist industry, and can only be expunged in blood. Large numbers of Cornishmen feel, in their turn, that if that's the way it has to be, then it's all right with them; rancour still smoulders at the memory of Cornwall's defeat in 838 at the hands of King Egbert, who invaded the country from Devon with a mob of Viking tearaways and opened it up to English settlers. The huge Cornish sales of *The Carpetbaggers* were entirely due to the belief that the book dealt sympathetically with the desecration wrought by Egbert's followers; the discovery that this wasn't the case only served to exacerbate the situation, confirming the eternal Cornish suspicion that Englishmen live only for the chance to put one over on them.

Urban Cornwall, however, has come to grudging terms with its proximity to England. Penzance, after all, is best-known as the terminus of the old Great Western Railway. It also contains an antiquarian bookshop specialising in the literature of Cornwall and the Scilly Isles (a charming outcrop, famous chiefly for flowers and Harold Wilson, a combination which fortunately defies description). Penzance, whose rateable value of £637,099 levied at 10/2 in the £ compares favourably with any in the land, is a centre of the gnome industry. From the thriving kilns of thousands of Cornish potters, gnomes, pelicans, tortoises, sundials, and lumps of rock cunningly worked and shaped to look like lumps of rock are brought to the railhead at Penzance for shipment to all parts of the country. Suburbia owes a great debt to these craftsmen; it is too often forgotten that, without them, children in Guildford and Hendon might never have seen a penguin at all. Art, in fact, is Cornwall's primary industry: to date, the bay of St Ives has earned almost three million dollars in pictorial dishcloths alone, and if all the paintings of St. Michael's Mount at sunrise were placed end to end along the M1, the world would be a better place. Villages like Polperro expanded up hillsides solely in order that their inhabitants could take better photographs of the bays below for sale to postcard concessionaires; through sheer good fortune, these hills have themselves become profitably graphic by-products. Non-fishing is also an important source of revenue to these little ports; at the drop of an American Express traveller's cheque, non fisherman can be persuaded to pose alongside children, wives, mothers-in-law, to crouch Cornishly beside lobster pots and permanently unmended nets, or simply to stand in their non-fishing boats with one oar over their shoulder gazing movingly out towards the eternal sea on which they do not rely for their very existence.

Truro's fame, of course, rests largely on its Anthony Trollope pillarbox in Quay Street, against which the novelist was wont to lean while composing novels before breakfast, and the town has justly become the administrative centre of Cornwall. Fowey, on the other hand, is the export centre for China clay, indispensable to the manufacture of stomach powders and lipstick; the stuff itself is dug out of the ground near St Austell, and unfair criticism is levelled at the city authorities on account of the filthy white slag-heaps that now fill the landscape; critics forget that some day, somehow, someone in St. Austell is going to find a market for slag, and strong men will fight to kiss the hem of his garment as he is carried through the streets.

Apart from these teeming conurbations, Cornwall is fraught with scenery, most of it round the edges; these are separated by granite moors, notably Bodmin, which reaches its zenith in Brown Willy, a tor rewarding climbers with unparalleled views of the sky. Further away lies Perranporth, the shrine of St. Piran, patron saint of the tin trade, who currently seems to be undergoing a low point in his professional career, to judge from the derelict workings with which the environs are dotted; and beyond that, Tintagel, traditional home of King Arthur tablemats, Merlin teaspoons, and genuine Tristan and Iseult bookends.

But the main thinking- and talking-point in Cornwall today is, predictably enough, its ruler. Due to one of those genealogical quirks to which all of us are prey, he is both Duke of Cornwall and Prince of Wales, thereby happily uniting the two areas in a great pan-Celtic union. Unfortunately, he is also marked down as the next King of England. How Cornishmen will face the coming nightmare of divided loyalties, only the years can tell.

To cross the border into Devon is to enter a different country. The grim, almost alien, landscape of Bodmin gives way to the grim, almost alien, landscape of Dartmoor; but these are superficial differences. Basically, Devon is much more a part of England itself; the distinction can be best summed up by saying that Devon dreams of the day when it will be able to send a team to compete in the County Cricket Championship, whereas Cornwall dreams only of sending in a Test team. Devon has no separatist aspirations, no indigenous language, no tin, no gnomes, and even its colonial ambitions towards Lundy Island have grown more mellow with the passage of time and the realisation that there's no money in puffins.

Historically, Devon appears to have spent much of its time as a sort of transit camp: recent centuries have seethed with native Devonians going somewhere else, and outsiders passing through. The sixteenth century all but depopulated the area of anyone capable of putting one oar after the other. It was almost as if Devonians had been waiting for an excuse like a Virgin Queen hungry for territory (all other appetites being subject to unwholesome gossip) in order to get away from home base. Hawkins, Drake, Grenville, Raleigh, eagerly accompanied by local crews, were off and going like the clappers as soon as the wind was right; why, who knows? (Except, perhaps, the women of Devon.) And a few years later, an even more disgruntled bunch, the Pilgrim Fathers, chose Plymouth as their launching-pad, as if to emphasise that it summed up the worst of what they were dissatisfied with. Even William of Orange, Dutch and therefore abnormally equable, landed at Brixham, presumably on the advice of equerries who believed in a baptism of fire; he stayed less than a week. Dryden, being a satirist, naturally loved Devon; whereas Coleridge, a more sober lad altogether, was born in Ottery St. Mary and never mentioned the fact for the rest of his life. (The Man from Porlock, traditionally held responsible for the collapse of *Kubla Khan* by bursting in for a quick natter while the poet was dreaming, never actually existed; he was merely a symbol created by Coleridge to point out how great a poet he might have been if only he could have exorcised his traumatic memories of the West Country.)

Devon, then, has had to depend on a transient population for its existence. Understandably enough, when plans for a maximum security prison were mooted in 1801, Devon leapt at this chance of maintaining a stable population and offered Dartmoor at a ridiculously nominal rent, completely undercutting every other tender; yet, despite the most rigorous precautions, Dartmoor still has the highest break-out rate of any prison in the country (these statistics were painstakingly unconfirmed at the time of going to press, however, and the author is willing to haggle). Realising, therefore, it's peculiar situation, Devon decided early on to cut its losses and consider itself merely as a place to visit, since which time tourism has become its major industry and life force. Stop any citizen in the streets of Dawlish, or Lynmouth, or Ilfracombe, make a noise like negotiable tender, and from under his Dacron smock he will produce hot scones, first editions of *Westward Ho!*, stone jars of cider, registered packets of mailable clotted cream, fragments of Exeter Cathedral crypt, fresh mackerel, and sepia postcards of weird quasi-athletic rites as yet unpractised east of the Exe. He will probably be leading a wild pony that has been in his family for generations, and can always be prevailed upon to sing a chorus or two of the fortunes of Uncle Tom Cobbleigh (his great-grandfather) in local dialect.

Architecturally, the most fascinating single feature of the county is that there are no private houses. Drop in by chance at any of the eighteen thousand thatched cottages that infest the landscape, and you will find Birkenhead or Lewisham coming down the stairs with a shrimp-net, or a Sussex child talking to its crabs in the bath. Most of the other architecture in the country has fallen to pieces, notably the Norman Castle at Totnes and some forty predissolution monasteries; serious efforts were, of course, made to install h & c, priv. baths, TV lnges, writ. rms. etc.' but when the conversions were found to be prohibitively expensive, the speculators cut their losses and sold the lots off in little bags to visiting Americans; Exeter, for example, possesses a fine Norman gatehouse, kept as a tourist come-on, but the rest of the old Norman town is now owned by a coach-party of Dupont Nylon executives who came by one April day and took it back to Redwing, Minnesota. Still,

Wortham Manor, a fine eleventh-century granite pile can be visited for 20p including tea. And a child can see Buckland Abbey for 2½p.

All of which explains far more satisfactorily than a dozen volumes of English history why Devon and Spain have always been at daggers, not to say grappling-hooks, drawn. Philip II's megalomaniac dream, after his annexing of Portugal in 1580, of a vast Hispanic holiday resort stretching from the Costa Brava all the way to the Algarve constituted the threat of a death-blow to the Devon tourist industry which could only be answered with steel and grape-shot. There can now, in view of the subsequent realisation of these ambitions, be little doubt that the lemming-like rush of Devonians to the sea in the sixteenth century sprang from a widespread fear for the safety of their guest-rooms and tea-shoppes. Certainly, they chose their moment of time, and grabbed it; the defeat of the Armada marked the beginning of the end for Spanish dreams. It has taken them four hundred years to regain the tourist initiative, and, naturally, things are again about to come to an international head, cloaked in a political guise. And Spain should tread with care; for, when Gibraltar, as it must sends out a plea for mercenaries with guts and honour, the men of Devon will once more rally to the call.

The Still Centre

If there is one thing more than any other which does not sum up life in the Midlands, it is the endless processions of Greeks making their way to Hucknall Torkard. You may come upon them any day, usually towards evening, walking slowly down the middle of the road from Nottingham, carrying the traditional Ordnance Survey Map, the bottles of rezina, the volumes of Thucydides, and singing the poignant sunset dirges designed to welcome the squid boats home to Koypolis, twelve hundred miles away. From time to time, they stop, and the men, clad in their picturesque, ambiguous kilts, dance together in long melancholy lines. On a clear night, you can hear their thumbs clicking forty miles away.

They are, of course, making for the grave of Lord Byron, just as English tourists tread the tearworn path to Missolonghi. The friendly Midlanders treat these strangers with the legendary hospitality shown to all immigrants who have return tickets, and much has been done to strengthen the ties between the two nations by these colourful visitors and their drachmae.

But if this tells us little, or even nothing about what life is like in the still centre of England, it does bring up the whole question of why a man should have chosen to die in a foreign swamp rather than look for a job in Nottingham. The Midlands is constantly throwing up such paradoxes; and as it is the nub and locus of all things English, to understand it is to understand the whole. Treatises on that nebulous property, the English character, lamely attempt to explain our eccentricities in terms of class, or behavioural codes, or climate; there seems to be a deliberate, perhaps polite, refusal to see them as diluted tributaries of that weird undercurrent of madness which rises from some Nottinghamshire source, and has run at full tide through so many Nottinghamshire men. Men like Sir Thomas Parkyns, of Bunny, a village five miles south of Nottingham itself; known as the Wrestling Baronet, he dedicated a treatise on wrestling, *The Corinth Hugg*, to George I, and when no one had the decency to translate it into German, Sir Thomas quietly went mad, and spent the rest of his life putting up small statues to himself. Men like the 5th Duke of Portland, who did nothing but build gatehouses on vacant lots around the county. Or Lambert Simnel, who got himself crowned King of England in Dublin, came to East Stoke in 1487 to claim his inheritance, and was pounced on by that humourless monarch, Henry VII. And it is surely unnecessary to remind anyone that Notts contains Gotham, whose inhabitants are remembered mainly for such rational contributions to progress as clocks without works (so that their owners may live forever) and a plan to catch the moon in a bucket.

Whatever the dark reasons for this galloping madness, they were enough to drive out Nottinghamshire's five creative talents – Byron (to Greece), D. H. Lawrence (to Mexico), Richard Parkes Bonington (to France), Alan Sillitoe (to Majorca), and Samuel Butler (to New Zealand). Even today, despite the National Health Service and *New Society*, Nottingham Station teems with young, bearded men with knobbly staves and old typewriters, all waiting for the train that will save their sanity and carry them directly to paperback rights and a bijou villa in taxfree Corfu. Why Notts is central to things English is, unquestionably, its power to drive its sons beyond its borders; foreigners, fed by the BHTA on an image of Britons as stolid, mono-syllabic men sitting under oak trees holding a cricket-ball and a thatching-hook, never seem to realise that rebellion *against* these leaden elements is exactly what made Britain great. And Nottinghamshire, lying like a great placid lily on its pupating sons, had the effect, not of aborting them, but of incubating them until their stings were honed, and the calm surface of the pond shook with their rippling exodus. It is immaterial whether or not Robin Hood existed; it is sufficient that legend saw fit to set this two-fisted ur-Marxist in a Nottinghamshire context. It was inevitable that the fiercest battleground of the war between Monarchy and Commonwealth should have been here, along with the bloodsodden religious debate given as its official excuse. Inevitable, too, that Linby should have been the point where Watt's spinning machines revolutionised an industry and a society, and where the Luddite counter-revolution reached its most wretched intensity. England has suffered four great revolutions: industrial, religious, social, and sexual. Nottingham had them all first. Oliver Mellors, be it remembered, was a Nottinghamshire lad – by turns bucolic and urbane, tender and randy, devout and profane, archaic and anarchic. Nottinghamshire straddles England and makes itself felt with a force and direction of which the gamekeeper would have been justifiably proud.

If Notts is a hotbed of rebellion and change, or just a hotbed, Leicestershire, to the south, is its exact antithesis: a cool, pastoral county, which makes boots. Its most famous son, Robert Burton, devoted his life to the composition of *The Anatomy of Melancholy*, and no one that knows the area has ever asked why. Originally that part of Mercia given over in the ninth century to the Danes, Leics remains under their pervasive influence, its inhabitants pursuing their lives with the diligence and attention to minutiae which characterises southern Scandinavia. The people walk the soft green lanes in their new creaky boots, eating the world-famous pork pies and matchless cheeses, thinking about irrigation, and pigs, and sleep, and God, and wondering how it happened that fox-hunting became a political issue. Life moves at a peaceful lope, a long, gentle undulation, free from intensities of joy or despair. If *The Anatomy* is Leicestershire's magnum opus, Tennyson's *In Memoriam* is its most typical statement, and one understands the poet's motives in seeking out Shawell Rectory as a place to reflect:

> And gazing on thee, sullen tree,
>   Sick for they stubborn hardihood,
>   I seem to fail from out my blood
> And grow incorporate into thee.

A sensation, I am certain, that all Leicestershire natives will instantly recognise.

Given, then, that Leicestershire is a melancholic place, an area of flat, pale green landscape veined with sluggish grey canals and warted with ugly redbrick villages, and that it is populated with slow, reflective Danish emigrés full of cheese and sober thoughts, it is hardly surprising that a mad phenomenon like fox-hunting should have found here its fountainhead. Anyone who has spent any time in the chilling October mists of this flat land will recall how the languid pace of life, the dullness of the terrain, and the proliferation of gloomy philosophers can press against the temples and curdle the marrow. Against this background, the only creature which seems to have successfully overcome the weight of Leicestershire sobriety is the fox. Attractive, hedonistic, clever, parasitical, colourful, unproductive, irresponsible, he is a symbol of all that Leicestermen are not. And, as such, he is an infuriating irritant, like the chap you knew before you were married who is now a bachelor supported by beautiful women and constantly drops in to see you on the way to the airport. The fox, to all appearances, drinks life to the lees, and the only way around the perpetual insult which his existence provokes is to go out on a nice morning with forty dogs and a hundred chaps and tear him to shreds. If the climax of a hunt is not a pretty sight, it is only because the spectacle of the middle-class wreaking vengeance on a non-conformist can turn the strongest bowel. It is even possible to find hunters who conceive their sport as a divine mission; the fact that a layabout like the fox ultimately gets it in the neck proving that life can be made to conform to moral principles, if only the hounds get the scent of the malefactor. The fox, too, can be made to stand for any upstart daring to threaten the security of what is left of the Squirarchy; and it's more fun to get up on a horse than to stay at home sticking pins in plasticine models of Harold Wilson.

Since we are in the vicinity, it would be crass not to mention Rutland.

'One has no great hopes from Birmingham. I always say there is something direful in the sound' – thus Mrs. Elton, in a slander scripted with characteristic clumsiness by Jane Austen. Birmingham has long had to bear such taunts, and it has borne them with the staunch apathy which befits the home of Cadbury's Drinking Chocolate. Bournvita is the opiate of its people, and it must have gone a long way towards fostering that bland imperviousness to criticism with which Birmingham sits in the middle of Warwickshire on its great, fat, spreading rump. Warwickshire, the third component of the central Midlands, constantly lays claim to recognition as 'the county closest to England's heart', and students who ponder on our current arteriosclerosis would do well to examine this great gobbet of social cholesterol lying so close to our vital source. Not that its Town Hall does not possess the finest organ in the country; not that the Harborne Botanical Gardens do not smell sweet and blossom in the dust; and – what else was there? Oh, yes – not that St. Philip's Cathedral doesn't have four Burne-Jones windows; but it is difficult not to sympathise with the fears of men from Worcs and Staffs across whose borders the Brummagen suburbs had spread like semi-detached lava that will not be denied its diet of grass and trees and flowers. And yet, physical beauty is less important than the essential loveliness of soul which lies below skin-depth; if Notts is the quintessence of English *élan vital*, if Leics typefies our curious bucolic streak, Warwicks (or Birmingham, since the two are fast becoming geographically synonymous) contains much of that greatness of heart which the world is beginning to notice beating beneath our impassive British masks.

Earlier, I mentioned the four major revolutions which effected fundamental change in the social structure of this island, and the part played by Nottinghamshire in their development. But we are about to enter on a fifth, and equally significant one, and this time it is to Birmingham we have to look as a touchstone and example. And as a guide. *The Times*, with its customary foresight, circumspection, hindsight, and eye for a good subtle slogan, has called them 'The Dark Million'. They are, as it were, the maquisards of our racial revolution, that unnervingly rapid process by which Fuzzy-Wuzzy and Gunga Din, those big dusky children who used to ask for nothing more than a good scrap and the memorial of a few rousing pentameters, have suddenly turned up on the factory floors of their Mother Country. Understandably enough, it's all come as a bit of a shock to find that they wear ties, raise children, speak English, believe in God, seek love, work hard, use assegais sparingly, and think that the Commonwealth constitution guarantees free movement to all the members of that great big happy family referred to at 3 p.m. every Christmas Day.

Naturally, the county closest to England's heart has shown the stuff that made this nation great, and taken them to its benevolent bosom. Despite surprise that the new citizens don't seem to have learnt much about our ways from all those years of hobnobbing with the British Raj, the Kenya Police, the mining bosses, the Rhodesian farmers, and the friendly Nassau tourists, Birmingham has been quick to initiate them in our customs, and to integrate them into our society. Unions, employers, shop-keepers, landlords, churches, school-teachers, parents, and many privately-founded citizens' organisations, have all got together to explain to their coloured friends the difficulties of settling in England and to warn them of problems they may find themselves facing. At the last General Election, Birmingham and its suburbs took the opportunity of proving to the world that England considers the new conditions to be a serious subject, deserving whole-hearted attention, and the rest of the country has felt the pulse of its geographical heart, and responded with a speed and concentration of which we can all be proud. It is as if Birmingham, Warwicks, had said to itself: 'No, we are not Birmingham, Alabama. Nor will we ever be.' And those who know the tenacity, the compassion, and the feeling for England which the people of Birmingham possess, will readily acknowledge that any problems willl be ruthlessly exterminated before they reach proportions likely to disturb the sweet sleep of the Bournvita belt.

North by North-West

In the year 573 B.C., so the story goes, the poet Liun-Tsu was approached by one of the literary disciples with which the suburbs of Mukden were then overrun. Catching the old man by his sleeve, the boy asked a question of the sort which the world has since come to expect from the average Oriental lip: 'Master,' he said, 'what is to sustain us in our sadness?' Whereupon the seer turned his kindly saffron face towards the lad, and replied: 'We talk towards a golden land, into the sound of divine laughter.'

Liun-Tsu might, in his wisdom, have been talking about Lancashire; it takes more than mere geography to invalidate a dream. If there is one thing which sets this teeming sub-continent apart from the sobriety of Yorkshire, to the east, and the apathy of the Atlantic, to the west, it is its permanent atmosphere of comic riot. The history of Lancashire is written in hysterics a foot high; like Falstaff, it is not only witty in itself, but the cause that wit is in other men; it is the hilarious knockabout act on the end of the English cultural pier. And it never closes.

There is, naturally enough, considerable speculation as to when the joke actually started; some scholars become nervous if research is not pursued at least as far as the (probably obscene) joke about what the three Manx legs were all running away from; others agree that the whole business stems from a handful of extant Mercian graffiti describing conditions on the other side of Offa's Dike, built in the eighth century A.D. to separate Lancashire from civilisation. But whatever the primary sources of the Lancashire farce, no responsible academic would deny that its Modern Period began with the foundation of Wigan in 1246. Wigan was the first English city to be conceived as a basis for jokes; and it served bravely as the sole butt until the rise of the Victorian music-hall created an insatiable demand, to satisfy which Manchester (1838), Bolton (1838), Oldham (1849), Bootle (1868), and Accrington (1878) were all founded in double-quick time; since when the mention of their very names has been enough to send the coldest audience into uncontrollable fits and soften them up for the first real joke of the evening, which invariably involves a character with a similarly local name. Records show that on the first occasion when the name Ramsbottom was mentioned on stage, six men choked to death.

Not surprisingly, eight centuries as a comic prop has left its mark on the people; not just on their minds, or their attitudes, although these, too, have been moulded by the constant tides of laughter, but on their actual physiques and physiognomies. This effect has been intensified by social selection; while other counties have created folk-heroes with knotty arms (Somerset), barrel-chests (Suffolk), strapping thighs (Lincs), ruddy complexions (Kent), and so on, Lancastrians have taken a rather different course. Perhaps in no other area in the world could Wee Georgie Wood, Jimmy Clitheroe, Arthur Askey, or Davy Kaye have achieved greatness. Lancashire is a county where fathers pace the corridors of labour wards, waiting for news of a red nose, or ears like jug-handles, or a novel squint. Parents watch eagerly, prayerfully, for the first signs of projecting teeth, of a funny walk, of ginger hair, of anything that hints at the possibility of their offspring turning into another Ken Dodd. (Even when such ambitions are frustrated, the prodigy can sometimes get by on trust: the Wise half of Morecambe and Wise relies for much of his popularity on a phrase to the effect that he is 'the one with the short hairy legs'. The audience accepts this without evidence and laughs itself sick on the assumption that this is exactly what you'd expect to find if you looked up a typical Lancashire trouser leg.) If all else fails, the child is sent off to learn to play the violin execrably, to sing off-key, or to develop its natural accent to the point of unintelligibility. And considerable reliance is placed on clothes and other effects chosen carefully for hysteria-potential. A walk down the main concourse of a town like Blackburn at, say 5.35 in the afternoon makes *A Night At The Opera* look like a state funeral: pavements and gutters teem with tiny agitated Lancastrians in over-sized clogs, cloth caps, rosettes like dinner-plates, long mufflers, gorblimey trousers and collarless shirts. The incredible din, the manic hilarity, is not simply the result of an excess of luminous noses, squirting buttonholes, collapsible trousers, detachable plastic ears, and farting hand shakes; it goes far deeper than that, into that essential substratum of Lancashire life where something funny is constantly happening to people on their way to somewhere else. And the fact that, at knocking-off time, some forty thousand Blackburners are at that moment embarking on another eventful journey between loom and fireside means that forty thousand farcical situations are all germinating at once.

Of course, as with all complex and sophisticated societies, the working-out of these situations follows pre-scribed patterns and codes. The cries of 'Ey-oop, then!' or 'I say, I say, I say,' the pratfalls, the swift exchanges of hats, the removal of dentures (Stays, braces, glass eyes, toupees etc.), the wet roar of communal raspberries, the collisions with lamp-posts and busty girls, are all part of a ritual as rigid as a quadrille or a *suttee*; it is only *within* these predetermined touchpoints that improvisations can be practised. This element of automatism, of social con-formity, on which all such of comedy depends, runs throughout Lancastrian life. A pub, say, which does not have a resident Englishman, Irishman, Scotsman and Jew standing at the bar for the use of customers might as well close down; similarly, if the landlord doesn't make his daughter available to commercial travellers in the Snug, his licence is never renewed. And props like long woolly underwear, chamber-pots, parrots, bloomers, false bosoms, and spittoons are as essential to a successful landlord as dartboards and pickled onions.

Not surprisingly, all Lancashire relationships are con-structed along lines designed to elicit the maximum comedy from any given human situation. All mothers-in-law are

fat, warty, puritan and flatulent, and live in the best bedroom (the one, in more opulent establishments, next door
to the lavatory); all wives are belligerent, teetotal, avaricious and sexually neutral; all children either scream, or
throw up in charabancs, or, more usually, do both simul-
taneously; all friends are permanently sozzled; all enemies
talk with a suspect, simulated-southern accent; and all dogs
are old, loyal, brave and emotional, asking nothing more
of life than the chance to be epitaphised in a song, a little
song, a little song entitled *Just An Old Mongrel But Now
He's Gone There's An Ache Where My Heart Used To Be*.

Work, being a major part of waking life, has naturally
become the major joke. The Industrial Revolution, driven
on by such sons of Lancashire as James Hargreaves,
Richard Arkwright and Samuel Crompton, threw up as its
richest by-product the greatest stock of factory jokes the
world has ever seen. The whole complex labour-manage-
ment relationship was reduced to a ridiculous farce from
which it has little chance of recovering, since the organisation set up to effect a balance between the two forces itself
became a laughing-stock within hours of its inception.
Perhaps the most important piece of joke-material in the
whole history of Lancashire was the founding of the TUC
in Manchester in 1868. It presented Lancastrian workers
with a virgin field of comic situation and character, and
gave the world those imperishable heroes, Trades Union
leaders, Committee Organisers, and Shop Stewards. The
highpoint of any of the old *Workers' Playtime* programmes
was always the moment when the star comedian mentioned
the most officious, serious-minded and hardworking (i.e.
the most hilarious) shop steward by name; to anyone who
heard these programmes, the sound of five thousand mill-
hands falling to the canteen floor and rolling among the
tables will go with them to the grave. And it is almost
entirely due to the ravages wrought by Lancashire come-
dians on their own leaders that employers refuse to take
Trades Unions seriously. Unfortunately, employers are,
without exception, humourless men, the iron having been
driven into their souls by the fact that, since the Industrial
Revolution, there has never been anything but trouble
up at the mill. The Lancastrian upper-middle classes are

born into the pall of gloom that hangs over this knowledge, and into the atmosphere of angry fear caused by the mill-workers' refusal to treat the situation as anything but an uproarious hoot. The failure to break down industrial and class barriers in the North-West is a direct result of a three-way tension: labour is always straining to make new jokes about management, management lives in permanent apprehension of the jokes about to be made, and union negotiators exist in a state of neurosis from being unable to explain either the jokes or the gloom to the respective antagonists. There is little chance of the gulfs narrowing: about ten years ago, when England discovered sociology, whole busloads of field-survey teams took off for Lancashire; the net result of even the best of the assorted outcomes, *The Uses Of Literacy*, was to explain the North, rather inadequately, to the South, who promptly forgot; in Lancashire itself, of course, the Hoggart bit became just one more joke (the recurrent one about comic intellectuals with college scarves and moss behind their ears).

The apotheosis of the Lancashire joke is Wakes Week, which is a sustained shriek from start to finish, the noise centring primarily on Blackpool, Southport, and Morecambe. During this period, the cloth cap gives way to the cardboard copper's helmet, the headscarf to the celluloid stetson; black pudding is thrown over in favour of candy-floss, and the quart replaces the pint as the standard unit of measurement. It is a time of dodgems and lust, of hang-overs and winkles, of hokey-cokey in the Tower Ballroom and hanky-pankey on the sands. A Wakes Saturday night along the Golden Mile looks like an evangelist threat made flesh; Imperial Rome on the skids must have been very like this, the annual Big Dipper ride up to the edge of the ever-lasting bonfire, with Reginald Dixon playing Nero to the life.

None of which brings us to Liverpool.

For Liverpool stands apart, a city state, separated from its Lancashire hinterland by race, by language, by industry, and by mood. They do not spin in Liverpool, and consequently they do not joke; they lack the uniformity necessary for a background of sharable laugh-material. They unload ships, mill flour, crush oilseed, make bobbins, tan leather, refine sugar, pack tobacco, strain paint, bottle barley-sugar; this disparity, matched by the social disparity between the Welsh, the Chinese, the Indians, the Jamaicans, the West Africans, and the two brands of Irish, gives them nothing in common with the cotton belt; it doesn't even give them much in common with one another. And this is the real reason behind the Mersey Beat.

How anyone can mistake the teenagers' music, long hair, exotic clothes, habits, behaviour patterns, attitudes and morals as defiant non-conformism is beyond the comprehensions of Merseysiders. It may look this way set against the fixed generation-hierarchies of the rest of England; but seen in the context of complete social disorder on the part of Liverpudlian adults, the whole thing becomes instantly explicable. The older generation of Liverpool is black, white, yellow, brown, Hindu, Catholic, Buddhist, Protestant, turbanned, cheongsammed, dungareed, shawled; and it speaks twenty different languages and dialects. For youth, the only course of rebellion lay towards conformity, and if their standard is primitive, that's only because their society is in its infancy. Jeans are its fig-leaves, beat music is its ritual chant, and long hair, inarticulate grunts, solo dancing are its predictable characteristics. Banding together in groups of four and five for mutual protection and competition are its first faltering steps in community living. It is all, somehow, rather pure and beautiful. It is a civilisation in its infancy.

And it is the one thing in Lancashire we must all take very seriously.

The Mysterious East

What, exactly, is Orientalism? Is this word, coined by the West, used to describe a *genuine* property, a queer, ancient compound exhaled by centuries of *moo goo gai pan* and paper flowers and atonal songs and ritual suicide? Something tangible which comes only with vertical language and exploding populations and paddy-fields and gnomic poetry? Or do we use the word to label, instead, some artificial quality imposed out of fear, ignorance and superciliousness by timid Occidentals on a rather simple agricultural civilisation about whose human fertility the West has recurrent saffron-coloured nightmares? After all, Christianity is far more complex and mysterious than Zen; Wittgenstein more labyrinthine than Confucius; Joyce more weird than Ts'ao Chan; and quails in aspic more abstruse than prawn chop suey. Whence, then, the mystery? Whence inscrutability?

Anyone maddened by the apparent irrelevance of such questions to the subject of Ipswich and Beccles should take a large map of the world and hold it up to a bright light. It will not be long before he is thunderbolted to the quick by the physical similarities between East Anglia and China. No other country in the world is shaped like these two huge eastern buttocks of land; and, if the sheer weight of geophysical evidence still hasn't convinced the sceptic of the analogy, let him examine the way in which the rest of England considers its Orient. It is virtually identical with the world's attitude to South-East Asia.

Both countries have suffered from the Western assumption that physical isolation automatically means temperamental isolationism; the isolationism is, in fact, entirely Western in origin. And from this initial misrepresentation springs the familiar bifurcated attitude that what you do not understand must be either (a) mysteriously sinister or (b) hysterically funny. So into the joke-books of a billion Occidental Joe Millers goes the hilarious paraphernalia of, in the one case, yellow faces, sing-song voices, chop-sticks, rice-cultivation, pig-tails, comic peasants, and funny names (e.g. Hangchow, Nanking), and, in the other, red faces, rural burrs, clay pipes, turnip cultivation, tweed caps, comic farm-labourers, and funny names (e.g. Hockwold cum Wilton, Newton Flotman). As for the sinister aspect, this is also compounded of a thimbleful of half-digested facts, most of them topographical: East Anglia is seen as a great, flat soggy wilderness where bearded tits and bustards, not elsewhere found, croak and carol in the shrouding mists, where wild geese woo the moon, and where the sea laps hungrily at the reclaimed land it sees as its stolen property, held at bay only by the actions of witches, war-locks and tiny hunchbacks with sprigs of mildewed bind-weed.

The saddest feature of all this irresponsible myth-making is that the inhabitants of these countries ultimately begin to approximate to the myth-image; if the outside world seeks to impose exclusiveness and oddity on you, then you may choose, out of bitterness, to manufacture your own brand of separatism. And, just as China, for so long mocked and rejected, has responded by widening the rift from its own side of the line, so, too, East Anglia has come to separate itself from Mother England. The process there, however, started much further back in time.

In 400,000 B.C., to judge from excavations at such thriving knapping-sites as Whitlingham, there was little to separate East Anglian Man from his siblings through-out the uncivilised world: a stooping, hirsute knotty character, with scant frontal projection and a limited vocabulary, he was slow to anger; to almost anything, in fact, except perhaps to the manufacture of flint axe-handles, with which the area is rife. He also perfected the Small Round Stone, used for braining anything that wan-dered past the front of his hole. He was, in short, no dif-

5

ferent from the run-of-the-mill prehistoric biped. However, one singularly important fact must not be overlooked: at this period, England was still joined to Scandinavia, and the bulk of the population inhabited its eastern side; but there were extensive squatter settlements dotted around the rest of prehistoric Britain. These Western people remained a rather aimless, negative race for several eons; they left very few axe-handles or even Small Round Stones and consequently cannot be considered anywhere near as sophisticated as the East Anglians. During the Mesolithic Period, between 10,000 and 50,000 B.C., the East Anglians were knocking up harpoons, hammers, tiny jugs, and rude sleds by the gross; and still nothing was going on in the West, except the production of throwing sticks, and a few square rocks probably used for smashing anything these small, moronic communities could lay their fumbling hands on.

By 10,000 B.C., however, Britain was beginning to separate from the mainland of Europe; the lowlands between started to fill up, first with salt marshes, later with lagoons, and finally, at one horrifying bound, the North Sea. This transitional period was a time of great stress for Meso-Neolithic East Anglian Man; some threw in their lot with the Continent, and, as the water rushed over their stricken lake-dwellings, they began splashing towards Denmark, Holland, and so on. Many, not quite trained to make even the simplest decisions, simply sat there while the stuff slopped up to their eyebrows, pondering the futility of Neolithic life, and quietly perished. The rest plumped for England. East Anglia was born; but now it was a minority area – suddenly, the cretinous, brutish oafs in the Western sector were top men on the totem. Prejudice was born. It was 9,086 B.C.

During the next few thousand years, the West was filled with a slowly evolving race of power-maniacs, elementary arms manufacturers, and, naturally, fighters. Woad-covered gangs of Bronze and Stone Age tearaways roamed the countryside hacking one another to pieces with crude swords, spears and choppers, and generally despising the mild men in the East who were preoccupied with stopping the sea from dining off their families, and with developing primitive agricultural systems and fishing boats. In the West, the pattern of the modern world was being created in all its bloody malevolence; in the East, man was meekly cultivating himself into obscurity. The Anglo-Saxon take-over in the East was a peaceful enough affair; and the subsequent pre-Norman punch-up between Mercians and Northumbrians and West Saxons left the East virtually unmarked. They accepted Christianity quietly, happily; it seemed, in all its fine impossible idealism, to be just what they were looking for; of the extant one hundred and eighty Saxon church-towers in England, one hundred and nineteen are in Norfolk alone. It might have been our Paradise; we lost it, and perhaps that lies behind much of our scornful separatism.

Gradually, during the Norman Period and the Early Middle Ages, the gulf widened. The Norman temperament was totally alien to the East Anglian; London, which by now had become the controlling centre of the country, paid no attention to East Anglia, except to blow the occasional Middle English raspberry towards the rural Orient. Little by little, the men of Suffolk and Norfolk let the iron corkscrew into their souls; the practical, optimistic ones decided to cut their cultural losses and conformed to the picture the West was forming of them: sullen men with knotty fingers and a predilection for simple, basic things. They went away, usually alone, to cross-breed pigs and cows and sheep; many succeeded, producing the Large Black pig, the Dun cow, the Black-faced sheep, the Suffolk Punch horse; but many failed, and for years the country was infested with curious three-legged hybrids, miniature bulls, barking horses and hens that gave milk and went mad in the dark. Abortive animal husbandry created an even deeper sullenness and resent-ment in those sections of the population involved in the biological misery; it also gave rise to great waves of witch-craft, black and white, which, instead of clearing up the mess, worsened it. A village of some eight hundred souls in northern Norfolk became the disciples of a cow with two heads; when it died, the village broke up in disorder and its inhabitants scattered the madness in tiny dangerous fragments throughout East Anglia.

There was also, of course, serious revolt against the ridicule from the West. In 1549, Robert Kett raised 16,000 men outside Norwich in order to force the King's hand in giving a square deal to the peasants, whom the King, a lad of twelve, had no doubt only seen in primitive panto-mimes and therefore considered to be an even bigger laugh than his elders did. After four thousand of the rebels were slaughtered, the rebellion folded. During the Civil War, Cromwell, a Huntingdon man whom many maleducated but socially eminent Londoners therefore thought of as a comic East Anglian, put Norfolk to the sword and the flame, merely in order to prove this particular point groundless. East Anglia has since been singularly unre-bellious, restricting its open resentment to small pockets of resistance like that of William Dowsing, the Laxfield Puritan iconoclast who spent much of the seventeenth century in desecrating Suffolk churches for the glory of the Lord, George Crabbe, who employed the bulk of his poetry as a stick to beat Goldsmith's rural ignorance with, and the unknown madman who hung the bells in East Bergholt church upside down for reasons best known to himself, and then vanished.

East Anglia is, even more depressingly, an area deeply involved with death, dying and interment, a taste observ-able in so many Far Oriental societies for whom living is a wretched process the end of which is the only cause for celebration most of them ever have. The reason probably holds for Suffolk and Norfolk too. These counties are curiously proud of their ancient barrows, cairns and pits, which, seen close to, can be bitterly disappointing for the tourist, looking as they do either like unsuccessful bomb-shelters or like amateur elephant traps. Worse, from the beginning of the Great Social Rift, most of the East Anglian upper classes spent their time in commissioning horizontal statues of themselves to be placed on huge stone sarcophagi, in which they could be laid to rest, safe at last from the sarcasm of the West. The one great literary genius of Norfolk was Sir Thomas Browne, who made a career from the incessant contemplation of death (or Death, as they like to think of it locally); he at least came to terms with the gloominess of East Anglian life;

but, inevitably, the oppressive mood comes through in such characteristically sour statements as 'Charity begins at home' (*Religio Medici*) 'For the world, I count it not an inn, but an hospital, and a place, not to live, but to die in' (*Ibid*) and 'Hercules is not only known by his foot' (*Urn Burial*). And, despite his desire for translation to a better place than Norwich, he was nevertheless clearly disturbed at the possibility of 'that unextinguishable laugh in heaven' (*The Garden of Cyrus*).

There really is no need to analyse what for want of a better word can be called modern East Anglia; everything is just as it was, a little gloomier, perhaps, a little more sullen, a little more fatalistic. The few optimists still pursue agricultural development, the ringing cadences of Turnip Townshend. Coke of Holkham and other sod-turning pioneers committed to faithful memory; the rest survive, and, each year, the really sour gather in small malicious groups on the Norfolk Broads to jeer at the aquatic inadequacy of the only West Anglians they ever get the chance to see.

It is not easy to predict how this slow, corrosive process will end; but it is just possible. Already East Anglia has put out a tentative feeler towards the twentieth century by building a fertiliser plant on advanced lines; but it has done this experimentally, half-heartedly. If the area is finally to be accepted as an unqualified (and, hence, uncomic, unmysterious and unalien) part of the country which for nigh on half a million years has looked on it as an embarrassment to England's dream of an industrial/militarist/progressive society, it must continue the conforming process begun, so recently and so very late, with the construction of the nuclear-powered eyesore at the pretty seaside hamlet of Sizewell. It must build in the image west of its frontier. It must bulldoze unlandscaped concrete motorways across its churchyards and village greens; it must envelop its quiet country towns in openplan developments, tinfoil supermarkets, haphazard skyscrapers, bingoleums, bowling alleys, Hotscoff beefburger bars, drive-in laundromats, black concrete bus-garages; it must fill its unprofitable, wildfowl sanctuaries with billboards, neons, gas-stations, dog-tracks, industrial waste, jerry-built council estates, half-planned factory areas, shoddy apartment-blocks, and death-heaps of rusting abandoned cars.

It must, in short, Wake Up To The Facts Of Life Today And March Shoulder To Shoulder With The Rest Of Britain Into The Glorious Future.

Border Territory

Faced with a situation which threatens to loom beyond its comprehension, the State of Texas possesses one cast-iron last resort in its locker: it stands up, as one man, waves the Lone Star flag, and cries: 'REMEMBER THE ALAMO!' As last resorts go, the world has seen better; but Texas has yet to find anything as universally applicable or successful. It regularly carried the day from the Halls of Montezuma to the shores of Tripoli; it sent men seventeen feet above the earth on the end of vaulting-poles, while all the world wondered; when President Kennedy was shot down in a Dallas street, it sprang to the self-defensive Texan lip like Pavlovian drool; and, no doubt, should Richard Milhous Nixon find it necessary to push a few buttons to keep the world safe for democracy, those three words will pass into the waiting universe with all the rest of the gaseous waste. It is the cry of strong men returning to the womb to read the writing on the wall; it is the cry of Border Territory.

Well, so much for Zane Grey, and good luck to him; no finer man ever drew ten per cent of the gross. He would have understood the badlands of Durham and Northumberland the way no Englishman beyond their frontiers can. He knew that bordermen are not like other mortals. Border country breeds them that way; it is Alamo country, conceived in fire and gore, and its natal memories are of battlefields, and enmity, and courage, and suspicion, and a brand of fine, brave stupidity you only get when two strangers meet and one of them has a better gun. Border country spends much of its working life as either a battleground or No-Man's-Land and demonstrating such nice philosophical brain-teasers as the bullets that whistle through Jerusalem, or the wall which separates the good Germans from the bad, or the bad from the good, depending on your geographical and political position relative to Checkpoint Charlie.

The image of the Geordie as a hard-grained suspicious man living in a society where the closed mind is a social prerequisite as traditional as the closed fist is not a figment knocked up by strangers in the manner of the East Anglian myth discussed at the last sitting. Northumberland has been border territory for two thousand years; Durham too, has shared the environmental lot of these hundred generations. It was no accident that England's first practical railroad ran from Stockton to Darlington, and no further, when another half-mile of track would have carried it into Yorkshire; George Stephenson was a Newcastle lad, and would not betray his birthright so lightly. Who knew to what vile ends the facilities for thus crossing the border territory might not be used? After all, it was less than a century since the 1745 rebellion, and many an octogenarian standing on Darlington Station platform in 1822 must have waited for the 8.15 with sombre misgivings stirring in his head. Nor might the gleaming metals have been appropriated by the defensive English alone – in Warkworth, in 1173, William the Lion of Scotland herded the villagers into the parish church and burned it to the ground. Bordermen could hardly expect to fare better at the hands of nineteenth-century Methodism.

But the toughness, the suspiciousness, the xenophobia of border natives goes back beyond Anglo-Scottish animosity to the period of Hadrian's Wall. Before the Romans decided that Britain had a definite Northern limit, what is now border country was just so much carboniferous limestone topped off with heather, from clumps of which various groups of comparatively primitive locals would emerge and bash one another as a way of life necessitated by the shortage of food and goatskins. These were apolitical skirmishes, largely non-racial, and looked on by all involved as part of the ineluctable 9 to 5 warp and woof. The Romans then arrived and dug a ditch called the

72

Vallum. This, they claimed (being political sophisticates), was not intended as a military fortification, but merely as a line of demarcation. It shared, however, with the later Berlin wall and the ageless children's game, the quality of canny provocation: That line we have just drawn between you and us is now *our* line – step over it and we'll bash your rotten face in. The onus is thereby put on the side not quick-witted enough to have drawn the line first. The Picts, unaware of what made the Roman mind tick, promptly stepped over the Vallum and got the big stick, after which they retreated, reformed ranks, and created the situation by which the Romans could claim as necessary the erection of a coast-to-coast wall, forts, barracks, deterrents and all the other accoutrements of civilised society. Scotland was born in spite of itself; and Roman Britain (i.e. England) came, naturally enough, to regard the Durham-Northumberland area as its front line, a scorched-earth region inhabited by cannon-fodder. Clearly, no self-respecting southerner would wander into the area; and the only way a Scot could do it was by chancing his arm with the legionaries. Gradually, the trifurcated hate and resentment built up: hate came south from Scotland, fear came north from England, and within Northumbria, an occupied territory, hated and feared by its neighbours, the seeds were sown. It has been a sturdy growth.

The Border Ballads trace the development of border separatism. If you will turn to page 314 of your *Oxford Book of Ballads*, you will fall upon a nugget of ur-racialism which, in its social, sexual and political implications might have wept from the pen of J. Baldwin. It concerns a 'faire flower of Northumberland' who fell for a Scots prisoner her father had taken in some battle or other; sold on the idea that this Celtic stud was going to carry her back home and marry her, she steals gold, horses, *und so weiter*, and as soon as the Scot is over the border, he delivers the unsettling line: 'For I have a wyf and children five' and rides off crackling into the mists. The faire flower subsequently shuffles back home to her father, who immediately comes up with the fatalistic punch-lines:

'You arena the first the false Scots have beguiled,
And ye're aye welcome back to Northumberland.'

It was a sentiment that fathers in Wessex were rarely
called upon to express, and fully encapsulates the pre-
dominant belief in border families as to which end of
England has the stick and which the lollipop. Northumberland still has the lowest rate of intermarriage between
its sons and daughters and those of other counties
(Durham excepted); and the general southern drift which
has affected so many parts of the North has drained these
two counties proportionately far less than, say, Yorkshire
or Lancashire, despite the relatively greater difficulties of
life in the North-East. Nor has there ever been much
cultural infiltration from the border; its language is more
exclusive than that of any other English region, its idiom
is self-contained, self-nourishing; it has produced no major
writers, no artists, no musicians; and yet it has a flourishing internal culture, a strong oral tradition of poetry and
legend and an army of oil-painting miners. The trombone is
ubiquitous. What did come south from Northumbria, however, was Christianity; or at least, the reconversion of
England, initiated at Lindisfarne in the seventh century
by St. Aidan. Nowhere on this island was more qualified
to disseminate a doctrine of love and peace and spiritual
commonwealth, which bordermen obviously saw very early
on as a fair alternative to the broadsword and the pike as a
means of getting together with neighbours; it was rapidly
adopted by the rest of the country, just as rapidly adapted,
and within four hundred years England was ready to march
eastwards and spread the gospel by means of the broadsword and the pike. This may not have been what St. Aidan
had in mind; it may also have been directly responsible
for the border's washing its hands of any further cultural
responsibility to the rest of the country.

Certainly, the rest of the country has never been too
eager to recognise any responsibility to the border; Lindisfarne may have been St. Aidan's stamping ground, but the
true cradle of English Christianity is more likely to be
found in the home of the Venerable Bede, a place whose
name will be remembered for as long as men accept that

betrayal was a fundamental element of Christ's career. Jarrow is the North-East's Alamo, if the parallel is to be not glorious victory, but heroism and disaster and an ineradicable memory. There were other names in 1931, names like Sunnybrow and Tudhoe Colliery and West Auckland and Witton Park, one- or two-pit towns, one- or two factory dormitories, which, to quote the conventional euphemisms we use to protect ourselves from reality, 'fell into an everlasting sleep' from which the North-East has been given little encouragement to recover. Between the callousness and selfishness with which England treated its border territory in the third century A.D. and the callousness and selfishness with which it treated that same territory in the twentieth century A.D., there is little qualitative difference. There is only seventeen hundred years. And one could hardly hope for progress towards sympathy in so brief a time.

After the Jarrow rebellion and its inevitable (given the Southern attitude outlined above) abortion, the border returned once more to its pattern of withdrawal, stoicism, and tight, internal life. It is unlikely that the bordermen expected much in the way of results, anyhow; they remained characteristically unvociferous during the later thirteen marvellous years of Tory affluence when nobody had ever had anything so good before, largely because it would have been foolish to expect long shrift from either Harold Macmillan or Alec Douglas-Home; the border had had long experience of the habits of gun-toting Scottish rulers, and no doubt it counted it a blessing that they weren't actually herded into crypts and ignited. To be fair to the Conservatives, they did give the North-East a Minister all to itself. It was Quintin Hogg, (Eton and Christ Church), M.P. for St. Marylebone. He had every sympathy for the plight of the North-East, and once went there to tell them so.

October 16th 1964 was a day of rejoicing from the Tweed to the Tees; trombones honked and sparkled in the streets, women danced, and strong men wept for joy. Not that the borderpeople, even then, expected the miracles which had not been forthcoming for two thousand years; but they believed that, somewhere in the bright morning

75

of Wilsonian Democracy, there would be ten minutes for them. Schools would burgeon, houses mushroom, industry boom, and Browns rush in where Quintins feared to tread. The corridors of power had begun to echo with accents which were, if not exactly Tyneside, at least a damned sight closer to comprehensibility than the tinny ring of Etonian Scots, and from these fine new lips, the promises fell like monsoon rains to wash away the thirteen years of drought. The rainy season was short that year; the land absorbed the water, and when it had finished, the structural alteration in the dust turned out to be minimal. Belts would be worn tighter, and the bright morning would have to be postponed; there would be a curb to public spending. In Birmingham and Dorking and Hampstead, the people groaned and bitched and threatened, wondered where their next expense-account meal was coming from, and tried to envisage life as a one-car family. North of the Tees, the bordermen recognised that they had no right to ask for preferential treatment to bring them into line with the traditional standards of the south, set their jaws, and put the Northumbrian bagpipes back on the shelf.

Three hundred miles to the south, a Mr James Callaghan said, with his charming smile: 'We must at all costs avoid a repetition of the 1931 situation.' All around him, the people furrowed their brows and tried to think what he was talking about. And, with that bitter irony which bordermen have learned to accept as one of life's basic premises, it was only in that part of England where his words had most meaning that they were least needed.

Semitopia

As the sparks fly upwards, Middlesex was born to doom. It came into the world like the bastard son in some second-rate Elizabethan melodrama, fumblingly conceived and born with horrid congenital diseases; and having done the appropriate amount of strutting and fretting, destined to quit the stage coughing, misshapen, maladjusted and un-loved. After years of the sort of Anglo-Saxon bickering typical of the era which invented the Civil Service, Middle-sex was hacked from Mercia twelve centuries ago or there-abouts. It spent a mere two hundred uneasy years in its original form; in A.D. 1000, Hertfordshire was torn from its hapless vitals, taking with it most of what was noble and of good report. For the next eight hundred years, Middlesex limped along as best it could, before being dis-embowelled in the creation of the County of London in 1888. Less than eighty years later, the broken, disillusioned remains of Middlesex disappeared forever, gulped into the Greater London maw. Had it, at the time, been able to speak, Middlesex might justifiably have croaked: 'I have done the State some service, and they know it' and expired with a certain feeble dignity. As it was, it just went, leaving nothing but a sad flotsam of old signposts, cricketers, and enamel motor-car plaques bobbing on the metropolitan tide.

The question, of course, that immediately springs to mind and lip is: 'Why should a dog, a horse, a rat, have life / And thou no breath at all?' It could be argued that what this country needs is more questions like that; it goes right to the heart of country patriotism and country pur-pose, and if for no other reason than that Middlesex should not have died in vain, it demands an answer. Will the next generation of the two-and-a-half million Middlesex natives feel a cultural deprivation, a loss of roots, and identity, and ethnic meaning? Indeed, will the present population grow into an embittered race, fraught with dispossession, and end up sitting around the simulated embers in their new amorphous Plastihome Developments, murmuring in low sour tones of the glorious days before the City came to Hayes or out to Edgware strode? Already, the protests have been lodged, the preservation societies founded, the petitions circulated; all across the lost county, from Staines to Enfield, historians, naturalists, sociologists and native sentimentalists are storing away the pitiful acorns of this society about to disappear into eternal hibernation – the quaint speech inflections, the porcelain ducks, the fragments of uncut moquette and formica, the low-flush lavatory suites, the chiming doorbells, the plastic roses, the wrought-iron gates, the stone herons, the luminous nameplates in which the imaginative effort of the people is concentrated – 'Fredeliza', 'Dunwanderin', 'Casa Mia', 'Welivere'. But these are merely the outward and visible signs of that inward and spiritual *élan* which reached its apothesis in Middlesex: Middlesex was the quintessence of Suburbia, the capital of Subtopia, and with its demise, the Subtopian dream comes to an end. When Greater London standardisation has finished its spread, when Middlesex is nothing but labour-saving ticky-tacky self-contained communities founded by Span and Wates and their neutralising confreres, what, exactly, will this island have lost?

To begin with, semi-detachment. The semi-detached house, of which there are more in Middlesex than any other county in Britain, was not just a habitation and an art-form, it expressed a unique (and uniquely English) attitude of mind. It stood for half-committal, half-friendliness, half-isolation, half-a-mindedness; it stood for wary circumspection, partial ambition, social compromise. It stood, in short, for the New Britain of the post-Victorian era; at the end of sixty glorious years, an Englishman's home had turned into his half-castle. (The very name *Middlesex* might have been designed for our new brand image.) This coincided with the rise of our newest class, a half-breed class, which might be called the working-middle, or lower-middle, which came to its semi-detached homes with a heritage of terraced tradition, with social mores and instincts learned over the centuries in row upon row of Mafeking Villas and Paradise Crescents; to these people, the essential class-lines had been drawn between the solid rows and the detached residences in which the upper classes lived. They aspired towards the ethos of The Larches and The Laburnums, and suddenly there was a half-way stage between the two, a Mini-larches, not one thing nor the other. And that was when status was born, in the semi-detached limbo between two fixed social situations; because status operates not between diametrical opposites, between social blacks and whites, but in nebulous intermediary positions. It thrives on gradations, on shades of subtle greys, on the differences between front doors, and cars, and the size of telly-screens, and school uniforms, and grocery bills, and Continental holidays.

With the rise to eminence of Middlesex in the 'twenties and 'thirties, all the pent-up urges and needs of the bulk of the British population were given their heads. So much that was fine and beautiful in the English character was suddenly released; the shared suppression by Them (the Upper Classes) bred and fostered in the terraces went; people were no longer held down in resigned contentment, unambitious neighbourliness, common bonds that never got anybody anywhere; they were suddenly translated into semi-detachment, into the marvellous stone and steel-windowed Siamese twins that throve in Wembley and Stanmore and Edgware and Shepperton and Osterley and Isleworth; families were locked together with their new ambitions and desire for self-improvement, in groups of two. It was you and The People Next Door, and the cry was Compete or Perish! It was a great and stirring era; for once, as in our finest and happiest wars, everyone was working to one end, striving to achieve a single purpose and that purpose was victory: everything from the clothes one wore and the food one ate to the education one's children received and the funeral one's parents enjoyed was channelled into the great and insatiable furnace of status-seeking. Men worked with a will in their offices and gardens, on their waste-disposal units and their car accessories, on their wives' appearance and their sons' achievements. And, always, there was the face on the other side of the communal garden-fence, the spectre with the new power-hedgetrimmer or the iridescent concrete gnome, the alloy-framed greenhouse or the two-channel TV. Men rose to the new antagonisms; suddenly, nobly, they were ready to shed blood over who the communal fence actually belonged to, whose tree it was that threatened one's hollyhocks, who had the right to wash his car in the shared driveway, whether one half of a semi was entitled to a rich-grained, chromium-knockered front door when the other had just fitted a wrought-iron and frosted glass masterpiece at enormous expense. Should one's Grammar Schooled daughter play with the Secondary Modern twins next door? How much ought one tip the postman, the dustman, the milkman, given the unknown fiscal quantity across the privet hedge? People at last began to think and feel – needing allies, they went further than their neighbouring enemies, sought support from the people down the road who were detached from this particular quarrel but who had a green front gate like yours and had had similar trouble over it with *their* semi-neighbours.

This will die now, with Middlesex. Already the multi-planners are at work, and whole tracts of the county are being razed and new dwellings are going up to suit the Greater London standard of the Universal midclass home. The aim, now, is a return to terrace anonymity, to non-antagonising sameness, to, above all, the profits attendant upon mass-development along predetermined and pre-costed lines. The New Ideal Homes developments, the Span- and Wates-type man-made communities have suddenly deprived people of the opportunities for competition and advancement that they learned and tested in the semis. However, these urges do not die; the semi-spirit lives on. Already, in most of these new artificial communities a social distinction is being drawn between the twenty three-bedroomed houses at £7,250, and the twenty four-bedroomed ones at £7,950, based not on the practical distinction of the extra room, but on the social distinction of the extra coinage. The developers may landscape all the front lawns, say, to a given size and formula; but in the back gardens, the recherché shrubbery, the expensive flora are pushing their heads up through the sifted and standardised sod in the eternal battle for social advancement. We are not a country to tolerate the standard car, despite its practical advantages, nor the standard house, nor the standard school; we shall fight them not for any wishy-washy aesthetic ideas, but out of the sort of individualism and enterprise and self-improvement that only money can buy. To walk through a modern development of the sort which will soon replace the semis of old, dead Middlesex is a moving and elevating experience; suddenly, from behind a bush will appear a little lad in an Eton kit, a living challenge to the Comprehensive children in the eggbox next door; we may see basketwork Minis and Rovers in privately-commissioned twin-tone regalia; through the ubiquitous picture windows we shall see all the rich Liberty and Heal's trappings, each empty bookcase more Scandinavian than the rest. Suppressed, harried, sidetracked, blanketed by contemporary terracing and universalised plastic tiling, the spirit of Middlesex lives on. London may attempt to foist its standardisation and even its dream of a foolishly uncompetitive society on the Homest of the Home Counties; but beneath the double-glazing, and the undersealing, and the deodorisation, the Subtopian, midclass, Middlesex personality survives, red in tooth and claw.

Where, then, does Hertfordshire stand in this battle for survival? Hertfordshire was, after all, cut from the sirloin of Middlesex, like Eve from Adam; surely it must feel some sympathy and understanding and regret, even if only from the view of Middlesex's death as a cautionary tale for Hertfordshire? No. The execution of her mother county came as an enormous relief to Herts. As with most parental relationships, that between the two counties has always been one of mutual mistrust and misunderstanding and enmity. Added to which, the semi-detached ethos has snowballed to encompass the way in which the two counties see one another; they are semi-detached counties, fraught with the competitive instinct, staring over the common border with a mixed expression of fear and scorn. Hertfordshire has always held the upper hand. In the midclass status-scale, enormous prestige is attached to the quality of the neighbourhood *in toto*; there can be little denying that Herts is a better neighbourhood; more prosperous, more imposing residences, more successful businessmen. It has tone. It also has that prerequisite qualification for social pinnaclism, a more rural atmosphere; it has more Green Belt, more open spaces; it has, in short, a bigger and better garden than that of its semi-partner, Middlesex. It has a piece of the Chilterns, for which Middlesex throughout the short bitter relationship between the two counties never forgave it, and it has rivers which actually look like rivers. Herts people are constantly claiming that they are country people, really, that they use London as a convenient shopping area, but remain sophisticatedly detached from its urban grubbiness and meanness of spirit. London is all right for Middlesex, and vice-versa; when the vice-versa was proved by the action of the Greater London Council, Herts was ecstatic. London's appetite would now be satisfied, and Herts would go free; more, the choice showed that Middlesex was considered more suitable for a continuation of urban sprawl than pretty green Hertfordshire. This was the ultimate semi-detached victory – Hertfordshire had been separated forever from the stigma of its birth. Detachment had been conferred upon it.

It was a great and wonderful day.

English Bohemianism is a curiously unluscious fruit. It does not belong in the great, mad, steamy glasshouse in which so much of the art of the rest of the world seems to have flourished – or, at least, so much of the pseudo-art. Inside this hothouse, huge lascivious orchids slide sensually up the sweating windows, passion-flowers cross-pollinate in wild heliotrope abandon, lotuses writhe with poppies in the rich warm beds, kumquats ripen, tremble, and plop flatly to the floor – and outside, in a neat, trimly-hoed kitchen garden, English Bohemians sit in cold orderly rows, like carrots.

In our Bohemia, there are no beautifully crazy one-eared artists, no *sans culottes*, no castrated epistolarians, no genuine revolutionaries, no hopheads, no lunatics, not even any alcoholics of note; our seed-beds have never teemed with Rimbauds and Gauguins and Kafkas and d'Annunzios and Dostoievskys; we don't even have a Mailer or a Ginsberg to call our own. Our Bohemia is populated by Civil Servants like Chaucer and Spenser and Milton; by tough-nut professional penmongers like Shakespeare and Dryden and Johnson, who worried as much about underwear and rent as about oxymorons; by corpulent suburban family men like Thackeray and Dickens and Trollope. And whenever an English oddball raises, tentatively, his head, he's a pitifully pale imitation of the real thing – Thom. Gray, sad, thin Cambridge queer, Cowper, mad among his rabbits, Swinburne, a tiny fetishistic gnome as far from Leopold von Sacher-Masoch as water is from blood. The private lives of our great powerhouses of passion, Pope and Swift, were dreary and colourless in the extreme, and Emily Brontë divided her time between *Wuthering Heights* and the Haworth laundry-list. And history, though it may offer our only revolutionary poet the passing tribute of a literary footnote, will probably think of William Morris mainly as the Father of Modern Wallpaper.

There was, however, one brief moment in this socially unostentatious culture of ours when we were touched, albeit gingerly, by the spirit of Bohemia. I am not (how could you *think* a thing like that?) referring, of course, to the Wildean shenannigans at the *fin* of the last *siècle*, which were the product not of an authentic Bohemianism but of the need to dig up a literature and a *modus vivendi* you could wear with spats and a green carnation: that Café Royal crowd was the first Switched-On, With-It Generation England ever had, and the whole megillah should be taken with a pinch of pastis. No, the gang I have in mind are the Lake Poets, who had, for once, all the genuine constituents of real adjustment problems, social malaise, illegitimate offspring, numerous tracts, a hang-out, a vast literature, and, most important of all, a date: 1798. And since at first sight, and for several thereafter, the Lake District, a sopping place of sedge and goat, seems as unlikely a Bohemian ambience as you could shake a quill at, much can be gained by examining the area itself; one can do no better than take the career of its most eminent son, a William Wordsworth, and relate it (as all the local tourist offices do) to every cranny, sheep and sod between Windermere and the Scottish border.

I realise, naturally, that the aforementioned bard left a meticulous record of all that made him what he was, but since all writers are extraordinary liars, poseurs, distorters, and self-deceivers, I have chosen to ignore most of his farragos and interpretations; and for the background to this chapter, I am not indebted to *The Poetical Works Of William Wordsworth* (5 vols. Oxford 1940-49), *Wordsworth: A Re-interpretation* by F. W. Bateson (London 1954), *The Egotistical Sublime* by J. Jones (London 1954), or *Wordsworth and Coleridge* by H. G. Margoliouth (London 1953). In particular, I am not indebted to *Strange*

Seas of Thought: Studies in Wordsworth's Philosophy of Man and Nature by N. P. Stallknecht (North Carolina 1945). However, I gather from friends in the trade that no work of serious scholarship is complete without a list of references and sources three times the size of the thing itself, so for devotees of this sort of *narrischkeit,* a fuller bibliography will be found sewn inside the lining of my old green hacking-jacket.

Cockermouth, Cumberland, was the spot where, on April 7, 1770, William Wordsworth first drew breath, and the location goes a long way towards explaining his characteristic lugubriousness. In the Old Hall, now derelict and seeping, Mary Queen of Scots was received after her defeat at Langside in 1568; her gloom was plumbless, and her host, Henry Fletcher, gave her thirteen ells of crimson velvet for a new dress. This could hardly have compensated for having her army trodden into the mud, but it ranks as one of history's nicer gestures to Mary. Nearby stands Harry Hotspur's house, contracts for which had just been exchanged when the new proprietor was butchered at Shrewsbury, in 1403, and within spitting distance can be found a few lumps of twelfth-century castle: this was captured in 1313 by Robert the Bruce, and spent the rest of the century under constant attack and bombardment by any Scots infantrymen who happened to be in the neighbourhood. During the Wars of the Roses, it was first Yorkist, then Lancastrian, and the catalogue of woe was finally brought to an end during the Civil War, when it was demolished by the Roundheads. A mile or so away, at Moorland Close, is the 1764 birthplace of Fletcher Christian, leader of the *Bounty* mutineers, and the 1766 birthplace of John Dalton, the physicist whose nefarious theories led ultimately to the destruction of Hiroshima.

Given this agglomerated misery, it isn't difficult to see how young Wordsworth could become aware, very early, of the general rottenness of intelligent bipeds, by comparison with whom the local trees, thorns, and general flora assume a commendable innocence. One imagines John Wordsworth taking his little offshoot on trots through the topography, pointing out the various scenes of butchery and nastiness, totting up the huge casualty list, and pondering aloud on the question of how long it would take that diabolical infant prodigy John Dalton to come up with a hydrogen bomb. It's little wonder that William decided early on who his friends were, and began associating with daffodils. Not that the idea of Nature possessing a mean streak escaped him, either; the news that Fletcher Christian got his comeuppance for interfering with the rights of breadfruit was undeniably traumatic for young Wm. – thereafter, as the *Prelude* indicates, he couldn't break a twig or step on a toadstool without feeling that the crime would be expunged in blood.

He went on to Hawkshead Grammar School, where little seems to have happened to him, except that he befriended a lad called John Tyson, who immediately died, aged twelve, to be later commemorated in 'There was a boy, / Ye knew him well, ye cliffs and islands of Winander . . . ' This drove Wordsworth even further towards the mountains and shrubbery, who were obviously bound to enjoy a longer life-span and weren't going to peg out just when William was getting to know them. This was now his period of greatest involvement with Nature, a time spent sculling about the lakes with which the area is infested and grubbing about in the undergrowth, one ear cocked for the song of earwig and slug, the other for That Still Sprit Shed From Evening Air. It rained most of the time. And, as the years rolled by and William grew to pubescence, talking the whiles to roots and knolls, he became more and more aware of humanity in general as a collection of blots and errors. One could rely on the crocus; every year it re-emerged from the turf, developed into its tiny, private perfection, and then quietly pegged out. And other mates of the poet, like Skiddaw and Scafell and Easedale Tarn, changed very little from year to year. But as the maturing bard pottered around Cumbria, he bumped inevitably into some of the area's human population, later immortalised and now available in paperback, who served only to convince him that after the fifth day, the Almighty's unerring talent for creating perfection deserted him: the life of Wordsworth the Teenager teemed with mad old women, decayed sailormen, idiot children, dispossessed cottars, impoverished leech-gatherers, bereaved lovers, unscrupulous potters, orphans, mutes, destitutes, and chronic bronchitics. Why the Lake District should have seethed with such sad misfits and sufferers to the point where Wordsworth never met anyone else is a question I gladly leave to medical historians or any similar forager with the necessary time on his hands. But I would just like to point out to all those scholars who have wondered why Wordsworth should have been a believer in metampsychosis, (that dubiously scientific process whereby souls pass on from one corporeal form to another as the subsequent mortal coils get shuffled off) that he quite clearly needed the hope it offered: souls inhabiting the forms of Lake District inhabitants were so unfortunately lumbered, that only the belief in their ultimate transmogrification into a hollyhock or woodlouse sustained Wordsworth's faith in God's pervading goodness. There is, indeed, much evidence to show that the poet would have given his eye-teeth to have been a clump of heather.

In 1787, he went up to Cambridge. Everyone drank port and spoke Latin, and the nearest Cumberland beggar was three hundred miles to the N.W. Wordsworth was desolate, left the university, utterly unnoticed, and took ship for the Continent. It was here that he burgeoned and ripened under the cucumber-glass of Italian culture and Gallic revolution, suddenly exposed to all that the Lake District was not: Bohemianism took root in the Cumbrian corpuscles, and in the general uproar following the coup of 1789, Wordsworth sang in the streets, went about with his shirt unbuttoned, and seduced the daughter of a French surgeon. Again, scholars have been baffled by the whole Annette Vallon business: why the mystery, the concealment of Wordsworth's bastard son, the failure to return with its father to England? What the scholars have in textual fidelity, they lack in imagination; even without dwelling on the unwholesome possibility that Wordsworth's boudoir techniques, picked up at secondhand from observations of Esthwaite sheep, must have left much to be desired, we can make a fair guess at Annette's response to the poet's suggestion that she accompany him back to the fells to meet Mad Margaret, Peter Bell, Old Matthew, and the rest of the gang. At all events, Wordsworth came home alone, and unable to face the quiet of the Lakes, took Dorothy down to Somerset, which by now had got a reputation for having Coleridge on the premises. The two met up. Coleridge had already collected a Lake Poet, Robert Southey, and together they had concocted a form of early communism which they called Pantisocracy, so that by the time Wordsworth fixed his wagon to their star, the nub of Bohemianism had been unmistakeably shaped: of these two ur-Marxists, Southey had already distinguished himself for his opposition to flogging, Coleridge was smoking pot and seeing visions, and the pair of them had been writing like things possessed. With Wordsworth in tow, the poetic output stepped up enormously, and in 1798, he and Coleridge hit the market with their *Lyrical Ballads,* and everyone took off for the Lake District. The years that followed were ambrosial for Wordsworth: at last he could stop mooning about and involving himself with the problems of the educationally sub-normal citizens of Westmorland and Cumberland, and throw himself into the serious business of Bohemianism. Night after night the fells echoed to revelry and pentameters as the wild poets of Cumbria entertained thinkers and versifiers from all over the civilised world. Scott came, and Lamb, and Hazlitt, and de Quincey, until the nights of riot and boozing and composition surpassed anything the literary world had seen since William Shagsper, Kit Marlowe, Francis Bacon, the Earl of Oxford and Robert Greene had all stabbed one another in the Mermaid Tavern, leaving the responsibility for Elizabethan drama entirely in the hands of a Mr. W. H. Grobeley, the inn's landlord, who subsequently wrote it to avoid suspicion falling on his hostelry. No visit to Dove Cottage, Grasmere, is complete without examining the outhouse where Hazlitt's father, a Unitarian minister of strong liberal views, attempted to put his hand up Dorothy Wordsworth's skirt, and at Greta Hall, Keswick, can be seen the faded, bloody marks following a fight over the rent-book by its two most illustrious tenants, Coleridge and Southey.

But ultimately, as it will, Bohemianism died. Coleridge left in 1809, went south, and died of opium poisoning. Southey became Poet Laureate in 1813, and took to wearing hats and drinking lukewarm herb tea. In the same year, Wordsworth became the Distributor of Stamps for the County of Westmorland at £400 per annum, and as befitted a civil servant, moved to Rydal Mount, turned his back on liberalism, and finally petered out in 1850, leaving his cottage to de Quincey, who hadn't touched a drop for the past thirty years.

Today, there are few reminders of those high and far-off times: the occasional grocer with the ineradicable Hazlitt family nose, or the Coleridge lip; fading graffiti on some derelict farmhouse wall, retailing bizarre local legends in the language and forms set down in the famous *Preface* of 1798; the empty gin-bottles that have bobbed on Ullswater and Bassenthwaite for the past century and a half; a crumblng gazebo on the outskirts of Keswick, built by Southey and from which he would pounce on passing milkmaids. Naturally, there are far more memorials to the more respectable aspects of the Bohemians' life and work, and during the summer, the roads of the two countries are filled with coachloads of people from Bromley and Philadelphia being driven to Gowbarrow Park to look at the descendants of the original daffodils.

The traditions, too, are dead. Not only is the local population conspicuously sane, sober, ungrieving, unstarving and totally unlike the *dramatis personae* of Wordsworth's records, the visitors are similarly unpoetic and unBohemian. They throng the Lake District between April and October in great tweed crowds; they wear sensible shoes, and corduroy knee-breeches, headscarves and duffle-coats, balaclavas and plastic-macs; they carry stolid-looking walking-sticks, and rucksacks, and notebooks for pressing bog asphodel and saxifrage in, and Aer Lingus bags containing tomato sandwiches and flasks of Bovril; they have rosy cheeks, and hearty, uncomplicated laughs, and sturdy calf-muscles; they eat ham teas, and hold sing-songs in Youth Hostels, and go to bed at nine o'clock to listen to the wind in the eaves. Or else they come in Ford Cortinas and Bedford Dormobiles, with primus stoves and Calor Gas and tents from Gamages, to take their children boating on Windermere. And every year, they pay homage at the verdant shrine of someone whom they vaguely remember as being a poet, or something, simply because the guide book has led them to his grave, and because all tombs demand equal reverence. So they stand, heads bowed briefly, in St. Oswald's churchyard, Grasmere.

Never for one moment realising that Wordsworth himself would have thrown up at the sight of them.

AMERICAN DREAMS

When the Kissing
Had to Stop

Sex, as the traditional preoccupation of American college students, is dead, says the Rev. Earl Brill, a college chaplain. It has been replaced by civil rights and war concern.
Daily Telegraph

Gently, an ivory disc of Californian moon rose over the dark knuckle of Bodega Head, striking soft phosphorescence from the still Pacific and picking out the slogans pasted on the flanks of a ramshackle convertible parked beside the highway. *HANDS OFF VIETNAM!* they shrieked: *BAN THE BOMB! LET MY PEOPLE GO!*

Behind the wheel sat tanned, cadaverous, liberal sophomore Wiley Folkenflik Jr., champion of civil liberties, archenemy of H.U.A.C. and Hoover, militant angel of S.A.N.E. and C.O.R.E., a man whose very name turned whole sororities white overnight. Where Wiley walked, suburban shutters slammed and Young Americans for Freedom turned their badges to the wall in fear and trembling. And female students, terror and fascination wrestling in their untested bosoms, watched, quaking deliciously, as his shadow passed.

One such maiden sat beside him now, Dulalia Freeport, blonde Baptist cheerleader, slim of leg and lush of texture, pure, smooth and tempting as an unnibbled peach, who dreamed of some day raising a son to be the first All-American footballer to put a chapel into orbit around Uranus. As she sat now, shrinking, beside the awesome Folkenflik, her soul cried out at her own folly: she had eaten his Tastee Whamburger, she had sipped his Joo-C-

91

Frute – but at what cost? What final reckoning?

In the heavy midnight silence, Folkenflik spoke suddenly.

'They're building a nuclear reactor up there,' he said, pointing. 'Don't you think that's a lousy thing for a government to do?'

Dulalia gasped. She bit her tender lip.

'Please, Wiley,' she muttered quickly, 'don't talk that way. I mean, I'm not that kind of girl. I mean, I think you ought to know that. If we're going to date one another. I mean.'

Folkenflik laughed, a dark, sophisticated, liberal laugh.

'Whyever not? Hell, Dulalia, you're almost eighteen. We're adults, you and I. Nuclear power is a fact of life.'

She looked desperately at the shining sea.

'I know, Wiley. But once a boy and girl start talking about – about peaceful uses of atomic energy, that kind of thing, well, pretty soon they'll be discussing – discussing *bombs*, or something. Or – or integration. It's how these things start. I've heard from other girls. You don't find out until it's too late. I think I should tell you, my mother warned me about boys like you. I mean.'

Wiley sighed a weary, experienced sigh.

'Dulalia, I want you to understand I respect you as a *person*. Not just another girl to discuss Red China with. They're a dime a dozen, that sort of girl. I want a *relationship*. There's nothing sordid about discussion, Dulalia. Why, your own mother and father do it, I'm sure – '

'Please, Wiley, you mustn't say things like that.'

'There's nothing to be afraid of. Discussion can be very fine, a very wonderful experience. A person isn't mature until he or she has engaged in political intercourse. Trust me, Dulalia.'

He turned his famous smile upon her, and she felt her knees dissolve. She found herself wanting to talk about civil rights more than ever before, but she forced herself to think of other things.

'It's this way, Wiley,' she murmured at last. 'I've been brought up to believe that people oughtn't to talk about Vietnam or Negroes or Socialised Medicine or anything until after they're married. Until they know what they're doing.' She looked down at her hands. 'It's always the girl that pays, Wiley. I mean, only last week Myra Duesenberg went out in a four with that terrible Morris Fisch, the one who's always handing out leaflets and everything, and they're in the back seat of this sedan, and it's pretty dark, and suddenly this Morris Fisch turns to her and says: "Myra, don't you figure we ought to negotiate with the Viet Cong?" And before she knew what she was doing, she'd replied. Well, right after that they pulled over to the side of the road, and they all started discussing. All *four* of them!'

Dulalia fell silent among her private fears. Far off, a fire flared suddenly on the dark beach, silhouetting the tiny figures beside it. Guitar strings twanged distantly, the strains of an old sweet protest song about the failure through union corruption of the Placerville artichoke crop. The music pricked tears into Dulalia's huge violet eyes.

'Oh, Wiley,' she murmured, 'just look at that dreamy moon!'

'It's too much,' he said, sighing professionally. 'And just think – that's the same moon that rises over the Da Nang peninsula.'

'Gosh, Wiley, I never thought of it that way. D'you suppose those awful Peking-trained Marxist lickspittle V.C. terrorists hold hands under it, just like us?'

'Depends on whether the war-oriented escalation-committed Pentagon lackeys happen to be bombing them at the time, I guess. Gee, honey, don't you feel that the unjustified strafing of Haiphong is leading the U.S. further and further into a position of confrontation that will make withdrawal ultimately inconceivable?'

Dulalia snuggled closer to the stringy arm beside her.

'Oh, Wiley, who knows? Maybe truce negotiations won't be possible until the Viet Cong are zapped to the point of accepting the impossibility of military victory.'

'But surely, Dulalia, continued bombing of North Vietnamese noncombatants will only strengthen their determination not to yield? Meanwhile jeopardising our chance of permanentising the Sino-Soviet split, and welding the Communist bloc more dangerously together?'

Dulalia felt her cheeks bloom with a new, exciting warmth.

'Never!' she cried. 'The split goes far beyond political considerations! It signifies the inevitable mutual alienation of Occidental and Oriental life-processes. Don't you see, Wiley, it's – it's – '

'Yes,' he breathed. 'Yes?'

'It's a RACIAL QUESTION!'

As the soprano cry rang out against the velvet night, Wiley Folkenflik Jr. turned to gaze upon the face of Dulalia Freeport. They stared into one another's eyes for a long, startled moment. And then the terrible silence broke on a single sob.

'Please, Dulalia,' he breathed in his lowest register. 'Please don't cry.'

The sweet shoulders shook, and the Beatle faces on her sweater grimaced weirdly with the sudden ripplings of the nubility beneath. Words slipped between her sobs.

'I – I'm sorry – I can't help it. I've never – I've never done this before. You – you do believe that, don't you Wiley? It was the first time.'

His fingers encircled her delicious arm, expertly.

'Easy, honey,' he murmured. 'The first time is always the worst.'

Dulalia brushed a hand across her melting eyes.

'I guess you've done it hundreds of times, haven't you?'

He shrugged.

'A few.'

'How many times, Wiley? I mean, how – how many girls have you discussed things with? Before me?'

'I don't know, Dulalia. But that doesn't matter. They don't count. It was never like this before. Never as good. Was it – was it good for you, too?'

She hesitated, afraid. She looked into his eyes. She nodded.

'I'd like to go home now, Wiley,' she said, very quietly.

As the dilapidated car drew up beside the impeccable anonymity of 146758 Chestnut Avenue, a light snapped on in an upper window.

'Oh, heavens!' Dulalia whispered.

'Shall I come in with you?'

'No.' The sweet chin dimpled bravely. 'I shall face them alone.'

'We shall overcome,' shouted Folkenflik, and slipped the clutch. Dulalia skipped quickly up the gravel path to face her environment.

Her parents were standing three paces inside the door, dressing-gowns over their night clothes, trembling between rage and apprehension. Henry Clay Freeport had pulled on his American Legion cap, for strength, and his wife at his shoulder, peering into her daughter's lovely face for a Sign.

'What kind of time do you call this, Dulalia?' cried her father. 'What are you trying to do to your mother and I?'

'Me,' said his wife.

'I mentioned you,' shouted Freeport. 'This concerns all of us. The family is the economic unit that made America great. And you,' he turned to Dulalia, 'have threatened the security of us all.'

Tears welled up in Dulalia's eyes, hesitated, and hurtled down her cheeks. Her mother leapt forward, enbosoming her daughter.

'What did he do to you?' she shrieked. 'What did he do to my baby?'

Henry Clay Freeport blanched, adrift in a world not his.

'Oh God!' he moaned to the empty air. 'And me a Rotarian!' Broken, he crept upstairs.

He was still awake, staring unblinkingly at the ceiling, when his wife slid into bed beside him an hour later.

'It was that Folkenflik boy,' she said. She blew her nose erratically. 'They talked about Vietnam. And the H-Bomb. And Martin Luther King.'

Freeport groaned.

'Will he marry her?'

He felt her shrug.

'Who knows?' she muttered. 'Who knows with youth?'

'Ach!' cried Freeport at the dark walls. 'There's so much goddamned youth about. Everything. Insidious. Threatening.'

'Maybe we should have talked to her earlier. About the Far East and I.C.B.M.'s and strategic proliferation, that kind of thing. Maybe we're to blame, Henry.'

Curious stirrings moved through Freeport. Things that decorum and practicability and middle age had long suppressed. He looked for a definition of his feelings towards Folkenflik, and found envy. It had been so long. His head turned on the pillow.

'Muriel,' he murmured, in a low, strange voice, 'how do you feel about Formosa?'

She started, snatched a glance at him, giggled girlishly.

'Oh, Henry,' she simpered, 'don't you think we're both a little old for that sort of thing?'

When It's Apple-Blossom Time in Orange, New Jersey or Abie's Irish Candidate

A Tale of Tears and Laughter, Big as all Show Business.

The whole story began (*said lovable yet cynical Harry Shoemaker, wizened stagedoorkeeper and Broadway savant who has Seen Them All Pass Through These Portals*) a long time ago, at the Downtown Greyhound Bus Depot at 7th and 43rd, on one of them spring nights, it's like you can smell something in the air, you don't know what. I'm just kind of standing around, chewing the fat with Nat 'Nat Lebncwicz (the great Yonkers ex-welterweight turned knish factor), when this bus pulls in from Nowhere, Iowa, and about nine million members of the International Hayseed Set get out and start running around looking for gold sidewalks.

The last one out is this kid in a green seersucker suit and yellow spats, and one of them red spotted bow ties, it looks like you got toadstools growing out of your throat, and a natty line in Iowa straw boaters draped over his brain like it was the first hat he ever wore, which it probably was. He's carrying a battered trunk with what must be his old man's initials on the side, kind of faded, and a pennant from Idiot High, and packet of jelly sandwiches, and a beat-up ukele-case, and his eyes are rolling in his face like marbles in a soup-dish. He hands his trunk to this Puerto Rican who's carrying a sign saying 'Portar' and a sawn-off scatter-gun, and the P.R. takes off uptown, destination unknown, leaving the kid grinning at an elderly bum who's just sold him the Lincoln Centre at the knock-

7

down drag-out price of fourteen bucks, which turns out to be all the kid has in the world.

'Gee, fancy meeting Leonard Bernstein on my first day!' says the seed, as I push through a line of drunks waiting to sell him the Chrysler Building and sundry other goodies, 'I always told the folks back home in Cornpone, Iowa (pop. 643, elev. 191 feet) I'd make good. What'll they say when they hear I bought the famous Lincoln Centre for only fourteen dollars?'

'They'll figure you're a pretty lousy businessman,' I tell him. 'The usual price is ten.'

The kid looks somewhat overcome at this item of news, so I take him to a nearby delicatessen frequented by Iowan showbiz personalities telling lovable old stagedoorkeepers about how all they want is to see their name up in lights.

'All I want is to see my name up in lights,' says the seed.

'What side of the business you in?' I yawn excitedly, figuring the guy is a conjuror or something, on account his suit looks like it's carrying hidden turkies.

'I'm a politician,' he says.

'Excuse me?'

'A politician. Oh, I'm nothing big so far, I mean, not a Senator or nothing . . . '

'You could have fooled me.'

'Well, I did pretty good in high school debates, and, you know, votes of thanks to the ladies who made this clam-bake such a success, that kind of thing, and the folks back home in Cornpone, well, they all sort of reckoned I ought to take it up professionally, and my old man cashed in his life insurance, and everyone clubbed together to give me this big send-off, and the high school band came down to the depot and everything . . . and I guess that's it, really.'

I pick up my hat.

'Well, kid, it's been nice talking to you. I wish I could do something, I mean like I know a lot of citizens around and about, and if you was maybe the young Doris Day looking for her first break, or Benny Goodman, someone like that, well, it's possible I could put you on to something. But politics – I mean, like that's the toughest branch of the business to break into, kid. If you want the advice of an old man, you'll go back home to Cornpone, marry the girl next door, keep a few chickens, maybe bang the population up to 647 or 8, and leave it at that.'

The kid looks up from his malted, and he's got this pleading look in his eyes you don't normally run into outside of a Disney dog movie.

'Wouldn't you just like to hear one of my routines?' he says. 'I got them right here, and . . .'

I look at my watch.

'Well, kid, it's 4.30 right now out in California, and I have fifty bills riding on the last race at Santa Ana, so what with one thing and another, I guess . . .'

'Fourscore and seven years ago,' screams the kid, jumping up on his stool, 'our fathers brought forth upon this continent a new nation, conceived in liberty, and dedicated to the . . .'

I hit the door at a run. A political expert I ain't, but a guy don't need no Harvard education to tell this kid is no Abraham Sinatra; and that's a fact.

I naturally don't expect to hear any more concerning this item, but a coupla days later I am gumshoeing through Macy's hardware department when what do I see but the kid himself surrounded by a flock of blue-rinsed biddies at whom he is shouting the odds concerning The Eezeekutt Potato Chipper, a snip at 39 cents.

'Ladies,' he croons, giving them both barrels from them big cow eyes of his, 'before I begin to extol the virtues of this magnificent appliance, I'd like to ask you just one question.'

At this, the old dames begin to shuffle forward on account of maybe the right answer gets you a free weekend for two in Atlantic City, but instead of asking them what's the capital of Nebraska or anything, the kid takes a deep breath and hollers:

'ISN'T IT ABOUT TIME UNCLE SAM WENT IN AND TOLD CHARLIE CONG WHO'S BOSS IN VIET-NAM?'

Well, naturally, Macy's being the sort of establishment that stays solvent by selling 39c potato-chippers rather than free giveaway opinions, pandemonium breaks out! Two or three of the old dames near the front pass out cold, and the rest start stampeding for the exits, no doubt under the impression that the Cornpone Kid is about to run amok with his chipper and turn everyone into meatballs, and who could blame them?

The riot's hardly got started before the expected happens, and a floorwalker springs out of the woodwork, grabs the kid by the collar, and begins to propel him in the general direction of Iowa. The two of them are moving across the landscape at a fair canter into the kid's political sunset, when an old guy in a handmade suit suddenly detaches himself from the crowd, jabs his cane into the floorwalker's ribs, and cries: 'Unhand this gentleman!' The floorwalker takes one look, drops the kid like he was a long stick on a short fuse, and cringes back whence he came. At this, I straighten my tie and start strolling towards the centre of operations, on account of the old guy is clearly some citizen of standing and loot, and I do not wish to remain a lovable stagedoorkeeper all my life, thank you.

'Young fellow,' says the natty dresser, 'my name is George Hamilton Smiles III of George Hamilton Smiles III Electronics Inc.'

The kid is somewhat *gefrunzelt* by all these III's and things, so I step in smart.'

'Good to know you, George,' I say, 'I am Harry Shoemaker I, and this is my good friend, the Cornpone Kid.'

'Wilbur P. Gingham,' says the kid, shaking hands.

'Well, Gingham,' says G.H.S. III, 'I'll get straight to the point. I heard your speech, and liked it. Yes sir, I liked it fine!'

The kid reels back, and grabs my arm.

'You hear that, Harry? They like my stuff! Gee, I knew I'd make good in New York! Is it good enough to publish, Mr Smiles?'

Smiles claps the kid on the back, with some difficulty, since I am doing my best to get between them as soon as I see which way the cards is falling.

'Good enough, Wilbur? I'll say it's good enough! It's a new sound, that's how good it is. It's the sound people have been waiting to hear. Have you got anything else to show me?'

'Have I – ? You ain't heard nothing yet!' shouts the kid.

'Why, I got a speech about annihilating that there Red China, it's just about the catchiest speech you ever did hear! And then there's my anti-Medicare routine, and my keep-the-ghettoes-white campaign, and my Keep America Tidy . . . '

'That's all I wanted to know!' shouts Smiles. 'At Smiles Electronics and Missiles, we've been looking for the sort of candidate we could back, and back all the way. Let's talk business, Mr Gingham!'

'Shoemaker,' I say, very fast, 'Harry Shoemaker.' I smile, very modest. 'I'm the kid's agent.'

The old guy shrugs happily.

'Suits me,' he says, 'let's talk business, Mr Shoemaker!'

* * *

It takes me about three weeks to knock the kid into some sort of shape for the big time, what with showing him about lace-up shoes and how to eat off the knife and to spit behind his hand when there's dames present, and then feeding all the *megillah* to the papers about his family of Irish Polacks who came over with the Pilgrim Fathers on account of they wanted to be near Italian negroes, and how he goes to synagogue Saturdays and early mass Sundays and believes in big business because it gives a square deal to World War II veterans and All-American footballers, and by the time the three weeks is up, the kid's ready to open in Pinehill, Arkansas.

Now don't go looking for Pinehill on your map of the States, friends: it takes an expert to find it on a map of Pinehill. We open on a Friday night, worst night of the week, and the kid's way down near the bottom of the bill at the local PTA meeting, in between the barber-shop trio (I said it was a small town) and the announcement of the Little League results. Miracles we didn't expect; but miracles is what we get, and believe me, I seen 'em all, Judy Garland, Fred Allen, you name 'em. When the kid gets up and gives them his My-Uncle-Lost-His-Foot-For-This-Country number, I tell you there isn't a dry eye in the house. Right after that he hits them with his Anti-Income-Tax routine, and you can't hear the kid for the

101

cheering! He finishes with his God-Made-Me-White-So-Who-Am-I-To-Argue spiel, does an encore on his uncle's foot takes ten curtain calls, and they have to call out the fire department to cut a track through the crowd outside the stage-door! George Hamilton Smiles III grabs me as we hit the campaign car.

'He's a natural!' he says.

I smile.

'Can I pick 'em?' I say. 'Or can I pick 'em?'

* * *

That season, the kid goes from strength to strength; we play two hundred performances in forty states, and all the time the kid's getting bigger; more than that, he's getting known, every time he plays a new spot the curtains ain't open before they're shouting out requests. It gets so he doesn't even bother figuring out new numbers, the oldies go over so big; we play eight dates in Oklahoma with nothing but *Let's Poison All The Reservoirs in Cuba* and the chorus from *All I want Is Chiang Kai-Shek And Momma's Apple Pie*. It's right after we wow them in Springfield, Mo., that the kid buttonholes me, and I can see he's looking serious.

'Harry,' he says, 'I guess I'm ready.'

I look at him close, only I don't say nothing.

'I'm ready for the big time, Harry,' he goes on. 'I'm tired of playing these one-horse towns, these one-night stands. You're supposed to be looking after me, Harry, you're like a father to me. Harry, it's Election year. I seen them big stars, Nixon, Kennedy, McCarthy, all of 'em – shucks, Harry, they ain't but hogfeed!'

I look at George Hamilton Smiles III and a coupla the other backers we pick up along the way like Morris L. Shaw (Napalm) Inc. and Jack Rutt the Submarine King, and I can see they're looking kind of eager.

'He could be right,' says Rutt. 'I can smell peace in the air, and I don't like it. We could lose our whole advantage.'

'Strike while the iron's, you know,' says Shaw.

'Okay, kid,' I say. 'You're on. We open in New York, three weeks from tomorrow. Don't let me down, kid.'

I put everything I got into them three weeks, and most of what George Hamilton Smiles III and his sidekicks have got, too, which is what counts in this business, and pretty soon I'm able to tell the kid I got him this big spot at the Democratic convention in Madison Square Garden; not the biggest, naturally, on account of the biggest is already speaking, but the kid has a good pitch around the middle of the second half, enough to get him noticed and noticed good. And then, on the night, an hour before the kid's due to go on. I go around to his dressing-room, and what do I see but the kid sitting with his head in his hands.

'What gives, kid?' I ask. 'Not nerves? Not you?'

He waves a handful of cablegrams at me.

'I have to go back to Cornpone,' he says, sniffing. 'My ma got hit on the head with a pig, and my pa just heard he's got this Unknown Wasting Disease and can't work no more, and Ellie May Ginsberg wants me to marry her, and, anyway, Harry, I guess I ain't cut out for big-time politics after all.'

I fall back against the wall.

'Kid,' I tell him, 'there's twenty thousand people out there waiting to root for you! And two hundred million more at home. Kid, don't let 'em down! Don't let me down! Don't let Smiles Electronics and Missiles down!'

The kid shakes his head, and I can see his mind is made up. There's nothing more I can say, since I am not a guy who backs a loser when he gets the word before the race. The kid is already packed, so I pick up his case, and we head out for the door. On the way, we have to pass around the back of the auditorium, and the star of the show is making his act, and I hold the kid's arm for a second, and we both look at the stage and the guy in the spotlight.

'That could have been you one day, kid,' I tell him.

He shrugs, and sighs, and we're about to move on when the star suddenly stops, waits, and I hear him say:

'I shall not seek – and will not accept – the nomination of my party for another term as your president.'

I hear some show-stoppers in my time, but this beats all. The audience just kind of sits there, struck dumb. And then, from somewhere in the darkness, I hear this terrible cry, which I know from experience is the noise of a backer in agony.

'IS THERE A CANDIDATE IN THE HOUSE?'

I don't remember what happens to me after that. All I know is I'm pushing and shoving the Cornpone Kid down the aisle and people is crying and cheering all around us and the kid is trying to hold back and I'm waving at the stage and suddenly we're up there and the hot lights is on us and you can smell the crowd and you can feel the place shaking with the noise and I grab the kid close and I tell him:

'Okay, kid, this is your big chance! This is what you were made for, kid! Don't let me down!'

Silence falls. The audience is waiting. The kid kind of shambles forward to the mike.

'I shouldn't be here, folks,' he says.

Twenty thousand people weep.

'I wasn't going to run, I was going to Cornpone, Iowa.'

Twenty thousand people scream 'NO!'

'On account of my ma got hit on the head with a pig, and my old man got this Unknown Wasting Disease.'

Even the band starts crying at this. The kid puts his hand on his heart.

'I was going to go back and tend the chickens and marry Ellie May Ginsberg on account of she's the girl next door and my childhood sweetheart, and everything.'

The cheering and the clapping hits the stage like the surf at Waikiki, but when the kid holds up his hand, it stops dead.

'I ain't got nothing to offer. I just want to keep America the greatest damn country in the world!'

Well, folks, the rest is, like they say, history. I leave quietly after this. The kid don't need me no more. I'm just happy to see a dream come true, that any red-blooded all-American kid can get to be President.

And I do mean any.

. . . that Fell on the House that Jack Built

*'The bombing of North Vietnam has had little or no effect on
the flow of men and materials from north to south.'*
US Secretary of Defence McNamara

Five miles south of the D.M.Z., Major-General Sam
Kowalski, U.S.A.F., sopped up the last of his egg with the
last of his ham, sluiced it down with the last of his coffee,
and belched gently. It was good coffee. Not, he hastened
to remind himself (nostalgia being the better part of
valour) as good as the coffee in Topeka, Kansas, which
was the best coffee in the world. But good. He watched the
morning sun dissolve the white mists to the north, longingly: better flying weather than this, you couldn't expect.

Except there was nothing to fly against.

It had been that way for a week now. Daily, Kowalski's
reconnaissance planes went out, daily they returned, with
nothing to report. The photographs showed hills and
streams, trees and cloud shadows on the grass. Nothing a
man could bomb. Not even a goat. A goat would have been
something, thought Kowalski; especially a moving goat.
Now there was a challenge! Out of the amethyst sky,
Kowalski's spotless Skyhawks would swoop, hedge-high
over the dark grass, trim as white playing-cards flicked
across the green baize tables of home, and BLAT! No
more goat. One dead Cong goat.

Kowalski sighed, stood up, tugged his gleaming belt into
the soft movement of his breakfast, and notched it. At his
right hip hung a Smith & Wesson .45 Magnum, not Army
Issue, but Kowalski's own side-arm. His mother's Christmas present. She had gone into Duckett's Hardware in

Topeka and said did they have anything for her boy who was a Major-General in Vietnam, and the salesman had said nothing was too good for a guy like that and sold her the hand-gun for two hundred dollars. He threw in a hand-tooled cutaway holster, because that was the least he could do, he said; he would have been out there himself, he said, only he had had this trick knee, had it since he was a kid, gave him hell.

On his left side, Kowalski wore a Bowie knife. It was the sort of thing the men appreciated, he knew. It gave him personality, it gave him colour, it placed him in a direct line of descent from Sam Houston and John Mosby and George Custer and Blackjack Pershing. He wanted the men to know that if the Cong ever attempted to overrun the airstrip, he, Kowalski would be out on the perimeter, meeting them hand-to-hand. 'Remember the Alamo!' he would cry. 'Don't fire till you see the whites of their eyes!'

He walked out into the bright sun to where his Sky-hawks were drawn up, combat-ready, gleaming-white. Bullpup AS missiles hung beneath their wings, slim deadly, and Zuni launchers fat with 5-in. rockets, and AIM-9 Sidewinders, and plump napalm tanks like great grey footballs. Kowalski watched them through his smoked glasses, trembling with anticipation, feeling himself part of their functional mystery. Kowalski prayed for opportunity.

He was still there when the morning reconnaissance planes touched down.

'Nothing,' said the pilot in the de-briefing room.

'Nothing?'

'Looks like it, General.'

Kowalski flicked again through the blown-up photographs, still moist from the fixing-bath. He stopped suddenly, peered close, cursed the light.

'What's that?'

The pilot squinted.

'Some guy cutting wheat, I guess.'

Kowalski straightened up, triumphantly, looked at his assembled staff with bright eyes.

'Cong wheat!' he said. 'For Cong bread.'

A colonel shrugged.

'It's one peasant, General,' he said.

'Correction, Colonel! One Cong peasant.'

'North Vietnamese.'

'Cong, North Viet, what's the difference?' shouted Kowalski. 'He's cutting strategic wheat, right? To make strategic bread, right? To feed to Cong, so they got the strength to pull the triggers, right?'

Twenty minutes later, three Skyhawks roared off north. Sam Kowalski watched their black trails dissolve, willing them on, feeling in his muscles the faint recoil of cannon, seeing the shells stitch dark patterns in the earth.

Two planes came back.

'Who knows?' said the lead pilot. 'Small arms fire, maybe. I looked around, Harry wasn't there. Then I see this smoke, coming out of the trees. Maybe he just spun out. Who knows?'

Kowalski thought of the wreckage, the shattered wings, the dead engine, the wasted bomb-load. The Cong would take the tailplane and put it on a stick and take pictures of it.

'A million-dollar peasant,' he said savagely. 'Did we get him?'

'He wasn't there.'

Kowalski screwed the flight report into a ball.

'A trap,' he whispered. 'A goddam Cong trap!' He took out his gun and spun the chamber furiously while he thought. Also, he smiled, in a private, military way.

'Maybe the guy just went for lunch,' murmured the pilot. But Kowalski did not hear.

That afternoon, six aircraft took off on a seek-and-destroy mission to knock out the anti-aircraft sites. Kowalski had pin-pointed for them. That done, a second strike was to go in and silence the peasant.

Three bombers returned. The Vietnamese, having found themselves suddenly in a strategic position, had called up a couple of heavy machine-guns to defend their village, both of which had survived the attack that had homed in on the largest building, the school.

'School, huh?' said Kowalski, with a certain amount of relief, due to his having originally attributed the smallness of the bodies in the photographs to some fault in his aerial cameras. He turned to his wireless operator. 'Send this: Major-General Kowalski to U.S.A.F. H.Q. – In a preemptive strike against major supply dumps north of the D.M.Z., an A4F Skyhawk was downed by enemy fire. A retaliatory strike against anti-aircraft positions resulted in the loss of three further Hawks. However, a major V.C. training-camp was destroyed, with many – make that hundreds – dead. Ten thousand rounds of ordnance and one hundred tons of bombs were expended. Attacks continue. Message ends.'

The commander smiled triumphantly upon his staff.

'We got ourselves some war, gentlemen,' he said.

'For four Hawks,' said a captain laconically, 'they'll want results.'

'They'll get results. Tomorrow, we'll hit the missile sites.'

They looked at him.

'Missile sites?'

'If I know the Cong,' said Kowalski, 'and I know them, I can smell them, there'll be missile sites. They got the whole night to set 'em up.'

He was right. At dawn on the following day, twenty-four Skyhawks, heavy with H.E. and napalm, ran into a wave of North Vietnamese G.A.M.'s. Six were shot down, one crash landed in the D.M.Z.; two helicopters were lost trying to bring back the pilot, who died slowly, but was recommended for the Medal of Honour by Kowalski. It was good for morale.

'To the folks back home,' he told his men on the paradeground the following morning, and his voice trembled through the loudspeakers, 'that medal isn't just Charlie Fitzgerald's medal. It belongs to every man out here fighting for liberty, justice, and the flag. To your mothers and dads, and sisters and brothers, every one of you is a hero.'

The airmen shuffled their feet, and blushed. Some of them were very young. Pride welled up in them, diluting fear. Reminded of what they were there for, they climbed back into the cockpits in good heart, knowing that death could have a purpose. Pride filled Kowalski, too, as he watched them go.

'This is a major offensive,' he told his 21. C. 'Vital to the war. Strategic. If we break here, we break everywhere. But,' he patted his holster, 'no one's gonna break.'

That night, he went to bed happy. True, half his strike force had failed to return, but the day's sorties had racked up a tally of a thousand tons of bombs and rockets, which was a record for his sector of the front. Also, a large area of possibly strategic jungle had been defoliated, the district hospital had been razed, and innumerable chickens would not now find their way into the lunch baskets of General Giap and his friends. Kowalski, wide-awake, was still calculating the size of reinforcements he would need to call up in order to maintain his escalation at the prescribed level, when the first mortar shell hit the airstrip. Snatching his revolver and knife from beneath their respective pillows, Kowalski leapt out into the night.

It glowed bright as day. Burning fuel silhouetted planes for the few seconds necessary for their bomb-loads to explode, shells and flaming debris rained down, men in pyjamas ran about barefoot, shouting, firing at anything that moved. Kowalski, trapped by the twin agony and joy of war, stood rooted to the spot, gun cocked, breathing in the heady fumes it took two lieutenant-colonels and a cook to carry him away to a makeshift dug-out.

'I knew it!' cried the major-general. Beside him, a man fell dead, half his head shot away. 'I knew they'd have to come! They walked right into it.' His words were sucked away as an ammunition dump went up, tearing the night apart, but they came again ' . . . what you call war, gentlemen! Tomorrow, we'll get three divisions in here, four, we'll get two hundred Hawks, we'll get ground-to-grounds, and whole batteries of Lazy Dogs, we'll get nuclear . . . '

A grenade blew out the side of the bunker, flinging what was left of his second-in-command against Kowalski. The man looked up at his commander, dying.

'I wonder,' he murmured, 'I wonder – whatever happened to that – to that peasant?'

'What peasant?' shrieked Kowalski. He looked round wildly. 'What's he talking about?'

But before anyone had the chance to answer, and despite Mrs Kowalski's expensive Christmas present, they were overrun.

There's A Long,
Long Trail A-Winding

All along the meandering miles of duckboards flanking the Da Nang Road, the greasy rain pattered down, filling the trenches with thin slime until the corpses of rats and men floated free, to bob and bump like so many plastic ducks. In the icy dug-outs, the men played cards, or slept, or shot their trigger-fingers off aimlessly.

'We ought to fix up this lousy pit,' said P.F.C. Herman Topolski, 'We ought to clean it out, or something.'

Corporal Kristoferson spat over the top, and a Viet Cong bullet struck the spittle in mid-air.

'If you know of a better hole,' he said. 'Go to it.'

Topolski looked away. Through a tiny gap in the sodden sandbags he could see the same featureless landscape he had seen for the past twelve years: a few shattered tree-stumps, a few artificial hummocks where piles of his friends were melting inevitably into the surrounding slime, a few tattered limbs hanging on the old barbed wire.

'In case you were wondering, buddy,' said the corporal, 'We're here because we're here because we're here because we're here. See?'

P.F.C. Herman Topolski waited for the dawn barrage to begin, and thought of home.

*   *   *

It was a great day for Private Irving Greenfeld. The wizened old President had shaken his hand. Mrs Richard Nixon had kissed him on both cheeks and wept into a bat-

tery of press lenses. The massed bands of the U.S. Marine
Corps (though depleted by now to an elderly fife-player
and a one-armed drummer) played *The Star-Spangled
Banner* and above the crude dais set up in the overgrown
garden of the ramshackle White House, the flag itself
snapped, crackled and popped in the stiff Washington
breeze. The vast crowd of old men and cripples and widows
and orphans and industrialists applauded vigorously. When
the cheering died away, the President spoke, and his tan-
noyed voice boomed back off the blighted trees and the
peeling architecture.

'As the twenty-millionth G.I. to be lucky enough to be
sent to the great and glorious battlefields of South Vietnam, Private Greenfeld, will you tell your fellow-citizens
why your country, in this year of Our Lord 1979, is still
fighting this limited police action?'

'They gimme the freedom of the Coca-Cola plant,' murmured the soldier. 'They gimme a gold-plated bible.'

'To keep the world safe for democracy!' shouted the
President.

'To keep the world safe from democracy!' shouted the
soldier.

The crowd cheered and banged their tin cups together
and wept, and elderly, beloved Doris Day sang *Keep The
Home Fires Burning*, and six daughters of the American
Revolution carried Private Greenfeld aboard the only
Cadillac still in existence, and four horses towed it (all
gasoline having been requisitioned for the war effort) to
the airport, and the twenty-millionth G.I. was flown out
to South Vietnam, where they buried him two days later in
an unmarked grave because nobody could find his head.
He was fourteen years old.

*   *   *

In his bleak, decaying, unheated office deep in the Pentagon, General Curtis Haig Washington blew down his
speaking tube.

'What in hell's going on?' he shrieked.

'The lights are going out all over Washington,' said his
adjutant. 'It's the old ladies running the power station, sir.

111

They can't go the pace. Shall I bring in the candles?'

Four night-lights were set up at the corners of the map lying on the general's table, and the ten beribboned officers leaned over it eagerly, fingering the tiny coloured flags with military ecstasy.

'It's true!' cried General Hergesheimer of the U.S.A.F. 'We did advance eight yards last month. Look!'

There was much clapping, and General Curtis Haig Washington blushed.

'It's just that we're discovering how to counter the machine-gun,' he said modestly. 'Saturation. A G.I. in full pack can run a hundred yards in twenty seconds, during which time your average V.C. chopper fires sixty slugs. Ergo, if you send seventy men against each gun-emplacement . . . '

'It's genius, Haig!' cried his staff. 'Why, if we can only step up their springing speed, we may even take Hill 276 some day!'

'Every position must be held to the last man,' said General Curtis Haig Washington. 'There must be no retirement. With our backs to the wall, and believing in the justice of our cause, each one of us must fight on to the end.'

'They shall not pass!' cried Hergesheimer.

'Up, guards, and at them!' cried Muldoon.

'Kiss me, Hergesheimer!' cried Washington.

'By God!' cried Major-General Winthrop Rockerbilt III, 'This is what war is all about!'

*   *   *

In Times Square, it took the New York police a long time to put down the pacifist march. This was mainly because the policemen were all in their seventies, and their guns were old, and there was only one bullet per gun which they were supposed to save for themselves since the population had been expecting Chinese parachutists to land in Brooklyn for the past twenty-three years, and they might turn up at any moment. There had even been talk of Zeppelins, or some such.

The demonstration went on for five days, and when it was all over, and the forty high school students were all in the Bronx concentration camp, the *New York Broadsheet* ran the headline: COMMIES FINALLY DEFEATED IN OVERWHELMING U.S. VICTORY! And since there was no TV, and only a few very rich munitions manufacturers had crystal sets, no one ever knew whether it was the Viet Cong who had been beaten, or the Fifth Column, or the Civil Rights workers, or even the Chinese parachutists. But the news made them all very happy, and many of them broke out the can of Budweiser beer they had been saving for a big occasion, and smiled for the first time in years.

*   *   *

In downtown Los Angeles, the board of Grover Guided Missiles Inc. tore their hair and wrung their hands.

'It's this goddam war of attrition!' shrieked the managing-director. 'It could be the death of us. Nobody's bought a missile for twenty years.'

'They told us a war economy would make us a fortune,' moaned one elderly director, pulling feebly at his ragged coat. 'But all they want is conventional weapons. Was it for this we spent five million bucks on research? We got sold a dummy.'

The board nodded, and small bright tears ran down their raddled cheeks. They did not even notice when their last surviving research scientist crept agedly into the room. He held up a small glass retort, and squeaked. They looked at him.

'Mustard gas!' he whispered.

The managing-director leapt from his seat.

'At last!' he cried.

'I could've discovered it years before,' murmured the scientist. 'If only I'd had some help. If only we'd had some universities to send us some young blood. If only . . . '

'Cut that commie cackle!' shouted the board. 'How soon can we go into full-scale production?'

'Just as soon as the girls start rebuilding the factory,' snapped their chief.

'We'll have to move fast,' cried a director. 'This may all be over by Christmas!'

Outside their broken windows, just half a mile away,

the Los Angeles Opera House suddenly folded in on itself, and sank into a pile of rubble. Among the dusty ruins, millions of termites the size of rats reformed themselves into orderly ranks, and began to march uptown.

* * *

'If we have to devalue again,' said the President, 'we have to devalue again.'

'Do you realise,' said the Secretary of the Treasury, 'that this will put the price of a loaf of bread up to nine thousand dollars?'

'Then it's a damned good job there isn't any bread,' said the President. 'Otherwise we might have a commie revolution on our own back porch, if we had any back porches left.'

The wizened senator from Arizona leaned across and grasped his President's hand.

'You're a great man, sir,' he said reverently.

'Thank you, Barry,' said the President. 'In my heart, I know you're right.'

* * *

P.F.C. Herman Topolski slid his bayonet under the lid and peered into the tin.

'It's turnip lousy jam again,' he said.

New recruit Mary Jane Feiffer turned her remaining baby-blue eye on him.

'Is there any other kind, then?' she said.

Topolski crinkled his brow, and scratched his bald head with his left hook, and thought hard.

'I think there used to be strawberry, once,' he said quietly. 'Or was it cabbage? Anyway, it was before the war.'

'Before the *war*?' cried Mary Jane Feiffer, dropping her carbine. 'Heavens, Herman, you must be absolutely *ancient*!'

Topolski stared out through the sandbags, at the old familiar treestumps. Funny how blurred they'd grown over the years.

'That's right,' he said.

And We Won't Be Home Till It's Over, Over There!

*'Paramount withdrew its backing yesterday from the £3,500,000
Battle of Britain film because of disagreements with Harry
Salzman, the co-producer. The company felt that Mr Salzman's plans were not sufficiently geared to the American
market. He holds that it is very much a British story and that
attempts to introduce American characters would dilute it.'*
Daily Telegraph

'The way I see it,' said Mervyn Rappaport, 'it's first and
foremost a human interest story, right?'

The assembled Paramount chiefs leaned back in their
chairs and smiled for the first time in months. The murmurs of a dozen executive ulcers died away in the soft
darkness of their fatty tissue. They looked upon their new
producer, and found him good. Mervyn Rappaport had
a dark suit, for one thing, and a ten-dollar haircut, and a
small, discreet windsor knot, and a brother-in-law with the
Chase Manhattan Bank. He had graduated summa cum
laude from the Harvard Business School, and by the time
he was twenty-five, his advertising films for low-calory
vermicelli had won him a Golden Bagel and a very special
place in the hearts of Long Island real estate men. Also,
he made no secret of the belief that *The Carpetbaggers*
represented the apotheosis of film as art, and if you wanted
proof of this theory of celluloid aesthetics, Mervyn Rappaport would draw from his immaculate breast-pocket a
photostat of the film's annual takings.

Mervyn Rappaport took off his rimless glasses and
leaned forward over the executive table, very sincerely.

'Wars are about people,' he said. 'They're about people like you and me, and the kid next door and the grocer down the block and kindly old Mrs. Papparelli who lives over on First and Tenth above the Lithuanian Church. That's what wars are about, gentlemen, and don't let anybody tell you different.'

The Paramount chiefs thumped the table. Several wept openly.

'Also,' said the new producer, 'we in the film industry have a responsibility to the America we know, love and serve. People come to the box-office, they want *heart*. History they can get from books. Who are we, we should expect a family man to shell out two bucks just so's some arty-crafty film director can force ideas down his throat? For two bucks, a man's entitled to see genuine human conflict and dames in their underwear, right?'

Nodding shook the room. Rappaport's hands expatiated.

'The way I see it,' he said, 'the film' concentrates on a typical fighter squadron in the summer of 1940. The location is Somewhere In England, except for the flashbacks to Providence, Rhode Island, South Side Chicago, Riverside Drive, Redwing, Minnesota, Lake Tahachapee, the Florida Keys, and Osh Kosh, Wisconsin. The typical squadron leader is Uncle Tom Washington, tall, with this chip on his shoulder. They call him Uncle Tom on account of his being a Negro ex-kazoo player from Baton Rouge, who happened to be touring Kent with Mose Ratmeat's Ragtime Fools when Hitler invaded Poland, and he stayed on and went to be a squadron leader because he believed in democracy and the money was good. All the other guys in the squadron love him, with the exception of this hardnosed Old South whitey, who came over to join the R.A.F. on account of his family originally came over to Virginia from Leytonstone with Captain John Smith, and everything'.

'They had a lot of this racial tension during the Battle of Britain?' asked a shareholder, anxiously.

'It was there all right,' said Rappaport. 'Naturally, they tried to keep it quiet, but it was there.'

'Don't lean too heavily on it, Merv,' said a director.

116

'Remember, we got a duty to twenty million potential spade customers, and we don't want they should start ripping out the seats at thirty bills a time.'

'It's okay,' said the producer. 'The racial strife bit only makes it here and there. The real meat of the story is where Steve McQueen can't keep off the bottle and his wife freaks out with this Luftwaffe character who bales out into their allotment and she puts him up in the potting shed for the duration. It has this tragic irony, see, with Steve and all the rest of the guys thinking she's digging for victory and all that jazz and growing carrots for night fighters, when all the time she's really padding over to the cucumber frames and making out with Hermann Goering.'

'I didn't realise what was going on,' said a backer.

'Yeah, the other Hermann Goering was a fake,' said Rappaport. 'This one's the sympathetic kraut in our story, he couldn't take the whole Nazi bit, so Hitler made him this kamikaze pilot and put his twin brother in the Government, reckoning the real Goering'd get shot down, only not figuring he'd land in this allotment, see?'

'That Adolf Hitler,' said the backer. 'He thought he was so damned smart!'

'It just shows you,,' said an accountant.

'How come Steve McQueen's this lush?' asked a director. 'I mean, we got a responsibility. We don't want to suggest the Americans who won the Battle of Britain were a bunch of soaks.'

'Right,' said Rappaport. 'We establish early on what made Steve hit the sauce. It was when he was organising the relief of Dunkirk – he persuades Winston Churchill to transfer him to the Commandos for the weekend, which Churchill does on account of he wants to keep Roosevelt sweet, and Steve McQueen's sister is one of Eleanor's cousins, on her father's side – and Steve is staggering across the beach with a wounded Viscount on his back, when this grenade goes off, right near his crotch. Anyhow, a Roman Catholic priest – I see Charlton Heston, or maybe John Wayne – pulls Steve to a little boat and rows him back to England, and Steve's okay to look at, it's his groin's taken this beating, which is particularly rough on account of he's only been married to Ann-Margret two days when it happens. This is why Steve hits the sauce and Ann-Margret goes through the gamekeeping bit with Hermann Goering. It all ties up great! There's a fantastic human drama bit where Steve tells the whole crummy story to Harry Kowalski, the legless flying ace from Brooklyn; they discuss Wounds and Life and God for ten minutes, I swear it's the most moving thing you ever saw in your whole life, especially where Uncle Tom comes in and puts his great sympathetic black hand on Steve's shoulder and tells him about the time he got his head kicked in in Camden, South Carolina.'

'I like the Kowalski figure,' said a backer called Kaminski, 'I like Legless Kowalski, all right; a real all-American guy. I take it he's Jewish?'

'Strictly orthodox,' said Rappaport. 'Which is the basis of conflict in the sub-plot. Kowalski's mother, still young and beautiful, has come over to London to make soup for Cockneys and keep their spirits up, and it's while she's doing a singing tour of all the American bases that she falls in love with this Group Captain Sanchez, V.C., daredevil pilot with a Puerto Rican bomber squadron operating from Maidstone.'

'I'm glad you got the Spicks in, Merv,' said an O & M man. 'I was beginning to worry.'

Rappaport looked at him.

'This ain't Signor Antonioni you're looking at, baby,' he said. 'This is Old Merv.'

The O & M man hung his head.

'I'm sorry,' he murmured. 'I should've known better.'

'That's okay. Anyhow, Legless Kowalski is pretty cut up, what with his mother carrying this big torch for a Roman Catholic stud from San Juan, but Sanchez comes to dinner and it's Friday night and there's candles and everything, and Sanchez gets real hooked on Legless and they get to talking about God and it turns out that what really counts is that men believe in God and it don't matter how you worship Him, and Sanchez cuts his finger and Kowalski's finger and they got the same colour blood, and Mrs. Kowalski cries and says how she's planning to have these Jewish Catholic babies who're gonna

118

grow up in a better world when this lousy war's over, and we cut from that to the potting shed where Hermann Goering's just saying exactly the same thing to Ann-Margret, and while she's putting her clothes back on, we see where she's thinking that maybe by the time the war's over they'll have figured out a way of operating on Steve McQueen, because she really loves him all the time. And right after that, Squadron Leader Uncle Tom Washington saves the Old South whitey when some British finks pick on him in a bar, on account of they resent the way he's winning the war for them. And whitey sees the Truth for the first time, that when the chips are down, we're all Americans under the skin. We fade out on that.'

The Paramount chiefs looked at him. The eldest and wisest cleared his throat.

'You didn't tell about the war bits, Merv,' he said. 'You know, the whole Spitfire scene. The Few, and everything.'

Rappaport shrugged.

'Me, I reckon the average American audience doesn't dig paying good money to see planes and bombings and all that crap. They're sick of war movies. What they want is real life. Right?'

'Also,' said the accountant, 'they get all they want on T.V., what with Vietnam documentaries and everything.'

'Yeah,' said Rappaport. 'And they get it free.'

The Paramount chief's beamed at him. He gathered up the pages of his script into his shiny attaché case, snapped the bright locks, and left. The eldest and wisest chief sighed.

'There goes a real professional,' he said.

Is There Intelligent
Life on Earth?

'*It may well be that man will one day have to face up to the fact
that he is merely a member of a second-class civilisation inhabiting one of the Universe's less important suburbs.*'
Californian astrophysicist (Time)

In the lush fastness of their split-level Graeco-Moorish
ranchette, set on teetering stilts above the green Los
Angeles smog, the Grover T. Hackensacks were laughing
and weeping at the *Andy Williams Show*. Not just for itself
alone did they love it; it was terribly important for the
marvellous feeling it gave them of community with thirty
million other peak-viewing Americans, rich and poor,
from coast to coast. It was like being, as Grover T.
frequently reminded them, in some great electronic
cathedral: he himself did not exactly know what God was,
but when Andy sang *Moon River* in close-up, Grover T.
Hackensack knew that He would do until the right Thing
came along. Indeed, if there was one mote on the family's
reverent pleasure, it was the nagging awareness that much
of the country was watching Andy in black and white:
the Hackensacks were High TV, believing that the full
ritual ceremonial of 30″ colour and stereo sound was the
only way to worship, and that refusal to spend the requisite
dollarage on the latest and greatest American *Wirtschafts-
wunder* was a base heresy against everything their country
held dear.

They were joining in a spirited rendering of the Budweiser Beer song when the doorbell chimed. They broke
off, startled.

'Who on earth . . .?' cried Clytemnestra Jane Hackensack.

Her husband pressed a button on his white near-hide
arm-rest, and sat himself upright.

'But it's Peak Viewtime,' he said.

Their youngest infant, Dowjones, turned his flaxen head and stared at his father with great cornflower-blue eyes.

'It's gotta be niggers,' he said. 'They wanna move into the neighbourhood. Can I have first shot, Daddy, can I, huh?'

Grover T. Hackensack rose, nervously, from his chair, fraught with indecision: on the one hand, he recognised his duty as a citizen to protect his property at all times and at whatever cost was necessary, on the other, there was the awful question of who would step into his shoes at Bettalife Missiles Inc. while he was recovering in hospital from possible assault. He squared his insignificant shoulders at last, stepped into the plumlit hall, took a Number Eight Iron from his golf bag, and opened the door half an inch.

Hackensack, tensed for a hail of blows, relaxed. The figure on the doormat was a mere three feet tall. He was dressed in an impeccably cut grey herringbone smock, and his tiny arms and legs were perfectly proportioned; his head, however, was twice the size of a football, hairless, and very bright green.

'Yes?' said Hackensack.

'I wonder if I might use your telephone?' said the figure.

Hackensack hesitated.

'Who is it, Grover?' It was his wife, quavering, from the living area.

'It's a little green guy,' shouted Hackensack, 'says can he come in?'

She appeared in the hall, the three children at her shoulder.

'We have a sign up, Grover,' she said acidly. She looked at the verdant gnome. 'We don't want any,' she said.

'I want merely to make a telephone call,' said the visitor. 'I shall, of course, pay for it.'

'I guess it's all right,' said Hackensack. He opened the door wide, and the little figure walked in neatly.

'He's coloured,' said Dowjones Hackensack. 'He's gonna phone his lousy green buddies so's they can all come and move into our neighbourhood and lower property values and sleep with our women.' He turned to his seven-year-old sister. 'How'd you like to have eau-de-nil children, huh?'

The gnome ignored this. He was staring raptly past the group and into the living area.

'Fantastic!' he cried. 'You have two-dimensional television.' His three little eyes looked up winningly. 'I say, would you mind awfully if I had a closer look?'

Grover T. Hackensack beamed.

'By all means,' he said. He had spent eight hundred dollars on the set, and it wasn't every day that an outlay like that was vindicated. He led the way into the living area. The tiny man rang his wee delicate fingers over the frantic screen.

'I'm a collector myself,' he said. 'I just love these old things, don't you? The only one on Betelgeuse is in the Natural History Museum.'

Hackensack blanched.

'That, sir,' he said tightly, 'is the latest miracle of all-American electronic engineering. The company responsible has a ninety million dollar turnover. They offer a complete money-back warranty, and,' Hackensack smiled triumphantly at his wife, 'I happen to be well-acquainted with their chief sales-manager.'

The Betelgeusian was silent for some time.

'I see,' he said at last.

Belle Telephone Hackensack, eldest daughter and campus queen, stamped her pretty foot noiselessly into the immaculate carpet, furious at the dwarf's apathy in the face of so much splendour. Everyone she had ever brought home had reeled at the spectacle of so much money so tastefully spent. It was the most beautiful house in the world.

'You may not realise this,' she cried, taking the visitor and shaking him angrily, 'but all our windows are triple-glazed for warmth and silence and open and close by electricity. We have a Krushmaster waste-disposal guaranteed to destroy everything except string, a self-regulating purple pre-softened water, and on a clear day, you can see our beachhouse in Santa Monica.'

'How quaint,' said the gnome, the line of whose mouths

had been growing tighter at each new item. Had the Hackensacks taken the trouble to notice such things in other people, they would have seen that he appeared to have become strangely depressed. 'Tell me,' he murmured, 'do all Earthites live like this?'

The Hackensacks all smiled, satisfied at last.

'No,' said Grover T. happily, 'no, they don't.'

'Just the poorest?' said the gnome carefully.

In the long, thick silence, Andy Williams' devolumed voice tittered tinnily through *Pretty Baby*, while the elder Hackensacks clutched at one another for support, and the three children wept noiselessly into their tangerine Kleenexes. When their father finally managed to speak, his voice was no more than a hoarse, menacing croak.

'Listen, fellah,' he said, 'out there in my electric-eye-opening weatherproof three-car garage is a '69 custom-built Cadillac with Automatic Everything, an acryllac-coated 4.2 E-type Jaguar, a fibreglass-hulled eight-berth Playking ocean-going powerboat, and the finest set of . . . '

The Betelgeusian raised a tiny green hand imperiously.

'Please,' he cried, 'I didn't come here to listen to your hard-luck stories. No doubt you imagine I'm going to offer you some kind of financial aid, but I'm afraid you're very much mistaken. I must say, I'm deeply disappointed – my colleagues and I gave up our afternoon off to come here, you know. In order to make contact with some sort of advanced civilisation. Advanced civilisation!' The Betelgeusian threw back his huge head, and from his three oblong mouths, stereophonic laughter echoed around the room.

'Now you listen to me!' shrieked Grover T. Hackensack. 'You happen to be talking to a Rotarian, fellah. To a founder-member and now Chairman of the Bel Air White Citizens Council, to a practically scratch golfer, buddy, a man who's been to Nassau three times, first-class air-passage *both ways*. My wife was formerly Miss Clytemnestra Jane Taintfree, of the renowned San Diego Taintfrees, a fourth-generation genuine American family, believed to be Scottish White in origin. Several people close to the President have spoken highly of them. It costs me close on ten grand *per annum* to educate my wonderful clean-limbed children, whose bridgework alone cost more than the annual budget of Guatemala. I happen to employ ninety sub-executives and God knows how many semi-skilled operatives in my capacity as Chief Advertising Copywriter for Bettalife Missile Inc., see?'

The gnome examined his fingernails.

'Missiles?' he said.

Hackensack smiled, nodding vigorously.

'I thought that'd get to you,' he shouted. He turned, still nodding to his family. 'I thought that'd get him. Yeah, fellah, m-i-s-s-i-l-e-s. It may interest you to know that right here in the good old U.S. of A. there's guys capable of buttoning-off enough nuclear warheads to wipe us all out forty times over. Right, momma?'

'Right,' said Clytemnestra Jane.

The little man groped in his smock and produced what looked like a cigarette lighter.

'You ought to use these,' he said. 'Cuts your destruction costs by ninety per cent. And no messy remains, either.'

The Hackensacks sprang away from him, but the dwarf merely smiled a smile of regret and resignation.

'I shan't, I think, be needing your telephone,' he said. And left.

Back in his snug capsule, he found his associates playing four-dimensional pontoon while the cook entertained them with quintuple fugues on his mouth-organ. They glanced up as he entered.

'Well?'

'Wretched,' he replied. 'Impoverished savages. Primitives.'

'Bang goes another intergalactic dream,' said the cook sadly. 'We won't be taking any of them back with us then, Charlie?'

The little visitor smiled a small multi-smile.

'I wouldn't say that,' he murmured. 'After all, we've got to have *somebody* to pick the goddam cotton.'

BEHIND THE CURTAINS

Mao,
He's Making Eyes at Me!

Love is a 'middle-class prejudice', a 'capitalist weakness', and a time-wasting 'psychopathic occupation', according to the latest Chinese Press pronouncements. In the Maoist view, married life is an opportunity for studying the works of Mao Tse-tung and maintaining a 'permanent atmosphere of ideological struggle and criticism in the home'. Attempts to reconcile family quarrels are considered unMarxist.

Daily Telegraph

Lao Piu-Fong was singing as he walked up the grimy staircase of his concrete apartment block. He was singing a song about the need to produce more 3.2 millimetre rivets, thereby prolonging the life of Chairman Mao by at least another two thousand years. He was singing despite the fact that a bus had just run over his foot and a rat had eaten his ersatz prawn during the five minute Thought Break at the factory and his best friend had been decapitated by the authorities for losing his spanner down a drain. He was singing, above all, because it was seven p.m. in Peking and five million people coming home from work were singing, and it was a thing it was wise to do if you had any plans about waking up the next morning.

He reached the scrofulous hell of the upper landing, where he paused to thank a kindly Red Guard for spitting in his eye and bayonetting his hat, and passed on into his tiny, dark flat.

Lao Piu-Fong had been uneasy all day. That morning, on leaving for work, he had failed to remember not to kiss his wife goodbye, which was something which always upset her. What made it worse was the knowledge that he would be unable to apologise to her, since reconciliation was also unMarxist. The only course open to him was to hit her.

She picked herself up off the floor gratefully, took his threadbare hat and coat, and threw them on the fire. Lao Piu-Fong bowed, and began singing a song about the shortage of glue in Maintenance Area Fourteen, and how it was directly attributable to the presence of Chiang Kai-Shek on Formosa. Then his children came in and swore at him until it was time for bed; the main target of their abuse was the fact that in order for him to have become their father at all, he had found it necessary to indulge in a spot of capitalist messing about with their mother, whom they similarly reviled for allowing him to pull his right-wing deviationist tricks in the first place. With happy cries of 'Psychopath!' and 'Warmongering Revanchist Tart!' they ran off to bed, leaving the Piu-Fongs despising one another in front of the fire.

'Excuse, most horrible fragment of dung,' said Mrs. Piu-Fong, 'but what is this I am hearing from many comrades concerning your filthy neo-Wall Street practices behind factory canteen with Worker-Waitress Eighteen?'

'Is vile slander put about by agents provocateurs for purpose of sabotaging output,' said Lao miserably. He sighed. He found himself unable to put his heart into vituperation this evening; much as he recognised his marital responsibility in reducing his wife to the level of a treacherous maniac, his mind kept wandering to subversive memories of lip and thigh. Tiny beads of sweat squeezed out of his forehead, slid down his nose, and splashed onto the thumb-stained copy of Mao's Thoughts open on his lap. It was not easy being a perfect husband. But he tried.

'Sickening poisonous capitalist toad,' he said, 'I am also hearing of your politically destructive laissez-faire policy with the riceman. What have you to say, dissolute cow?'

Mrs. Piu-Fong flushed angrily.

'Is loathsome lie!' she cried. 'Riceman T'song and I are merely discussing Chaper XVIII, paragraph IX – '

'SO!' shrieked Lao. 'While back is turned, you are considering question of leek-rotation with Riceman

126

T'song! While honourable first-class riveter husband is slaving over lathe all day, worm-eaten petty bourgeoise wife is sharing same sentence as pigfaced ricemonger!'

Mrs. Piu-Fong looked up at him, and sneered triumphantly.

'Now,' she smirked, 'we discuss cheap lousy middle-class jealousy of failed husband unworthy to sit in same room as genuine sepia-toned portrait of Chairman Mao, immortal father of his people. Please to begin, small thin dolt!'

Lao ripped his shirt, and began to keen.

'I have been jealous,' he moaned, rocking on his heels.

'True.'

'I have been possessive.'

'And worse!'

'Worse?'

'You have been guilty, unworthy morsel, of interfering in discussion of matchless gem-like Thoughts of Chairman Mao, and of attempting to subvert spiritual development of me and Riceman T'song.'

'Ah, so. I have been guilty of interfering in discussion of matchless gem-like Thoughts of Chairman Mao, and of attempting to subvert spiritual development of wife and Riceman T'song.'

'And?'

'And I have been having middle-class thoughts about female bus-travellers. And capitalist ideas about Postwoman Cho.'

'You are a psychopath.'

'I am a psychopath.' Lao Piu-Fong stared at the flickering grate. 'Mind you,' he murmured, 'I have not indulged in any perverted deviationist private enterprise for eight months. Is this not worthy?'

Mrs Piu-Fong spat.

'You are complacent,' she snarled.

'I am complacent.'

'Also you have been guilty of not repairing leaking tap in kitchen contrary to Chapter MCDXVI, sub-section IV, line II-V: *Urban progress possible only if each individual citizen-soldier recognises responsibility of maintaining roof placed over head through foresight and generosity of*

Chairman Mao. Similarly, you have neglected your duties with regard to faulty ball-cock, hole in bedroom window, and short leg on dining-room table.'

'All this I have not done,' groaned Lao Piu-Fong. 'Indeed, I am guilty of betraying great principles formulated on Long March.' His stomach rumbled. 'When are we eating?'

'First we sing magnificent chart-topper describing the joys of building new wing on public library,' said his wife. 'For has not peerless Chairman Mao written: *Hunger of soul cannot be satisfied with noodles*?'

'Probably,' muttered Lao, *sotto voce.*

After the song had died away at last, he looked down at his small wooden bowl.

'Excuse, please, obscene disaster in human form,' he said to his wife, 'but what is this esteemed muck I am supposed to eat?'

'It is from special Madame Mao recipe,' said his wife. 'With purpose of building healthy citizen-soldiers and at the same time destroying ugly capitalist greed-orientated appetite. Is sawdust foo yong full of nourishing synthetic protein, guaranteed free from artificial colouring.'

Lao forked a moist blob of the khaki paste into his mouth, blenched, and pushed the bowl away. His wife, poised for ideological advantage, raised an eyebrow.

'Well?' she said dangerously.

'Oh,' cried Piu-Fong, 'how all-seeing and talented is the great mother of our people!'

She narrowed her eyes.

'What are you trying to pull, revisionist fink?' she grated.

'Nothing. But see how my former fascist greed and un-Marxist appetite have disappeared through the wisdom of Mother Mao! Not one more mouthful need I eat, so successful has her policy proved.'

Mrs. Piu-Fong threw down her chopstick.

'Do you refuse, therefore, to give me the opportunity of self-criticism? Am I not to be allowed to repent for my deviation from the recipe as laid down by Madame Mao?'

'No,' said Lao. A tiny gloat ran across his lips. But it was short-lived.

'So!' cried his wife. 'Can it be, subversive louse, that you failed to notice the forbidden bean-curd, introduced by me for the sole purpose of testing your awareness of Madame Mao's edicts?'

A sob shook the mean little room. Broken, Lao Pui-Fong pushed back his stool and stood up raggedly, and bowed a small, pitiful bow.

'Am going to bed,' he said hoarsely. 'Am going to bed for purpose of self-castigation. Am indeed an unworthy husband and dialectician. So sorry.'

And, leaving her smiling terribly at the portrait on the wall, he trudged into the neighbouring room and threw himself upon the unyielding palliasse.

But self-criticism would not come, no matter how hard he tried. Each time he began to enumerate his deviations, slim bodies danced out of his memory and writhed before him, a thousand faces rose up from his imagination to smile and kiss, a thousand slim, seductive hands reached for his unworthy flesh. Until, at last, the incorrigible capitalist spirit of Citizen-Soldier Lao Piu-Fong fell into restless slumber, to dream its dreams of counter-revolution.

Now It Can Be Sold

It was 4.47 a.m., Far Eastern Standard Time. Thin rain hissed down the darkness. Somewhere, far off, a yang-yang bird shrieked, once, trapped by its own insatiable lust. The southernmost rim of China lay otherwise in the moonlessness; but through it, invisible, a very old lady was pushing a wheelbarrow containing an epidiascope and an ancient Remington typewriter towards Hong Kong.

Suddenly, as was its habit, the dawn came up like thunder. In the new light, a Red Chinese border sentry noticed the hobbling crone, shook himself free from dreams of glue and anarchy, and loosed off a couple of rounds. The bullets spanged off the wheelbarrow, but the human fragment between the shafts wavered not an instant. She put her head down and scuttled over the line, into Hong Kong.

'Good morning,' said the Customs Officer. A ricochet spun his cap across the room. 'Would you mind reading this card, madam?'

'So sorry?'

The Customs Officer sighed.

'Have you any barometers, cuckoo clocks, perfume, raw meat, narcotics, potted plants, Old Masters, cameras or animals?'

'So sorry,' said the old lady again. 'Have only most elderly epidiascope, secondhand, bills to show, also one upright Remington typewriter, also complete change underwear.'

'I see. I wonder if you'd be kind enough to tell me the purpose of your visit? That is, are you here on business, tourism, or perhaps – '

130

'Am Auntie Fu.'

'What?'

'Am Auntie Fu.' The crone bowed slightly from the waist. 'Am famous aunt of Chairman Mao. Am defecting to West.'

A tiny red flicker played about the Customs Officer's pupils, and a thin blue vein pulsed in his temple, like an epileptic worm.

'Would you mind waiting there a moment, madam?' he said.

He vanished through a hardboard door, into an inner office. A telephone bell jangled. Time passed, full of his jabbering voice. The phone tinkled again. After about five minutes, the man reappeared, flushed and flourishing a sheet of foolscap paper.

'I wonder,' he cried, 'if you'd be good enough to sign this trivial slip of official paper, madam? It's just regul– '

But Auntie Fu had snatched the thing from him, and, jamming a jeweller's glass into her left eye, she began scrutinising it line by line. At last, she flung it aside.

'Excuse, please, but you think Auntie Fu some kind of nut? This say it are contract for Auntie Fu memoirs, all world lights, one hundred pounds advance plus five per cent loyalty on all copies.'

'Oh, is that what it is, madam? Goodness me! Well, I shouldn't worry, it's best to sign these official things, it doesn't mean anything, you know, it's merely a formal– '

'Auntie Fu not touch anything less than ten gland down, used notes only, please, plus fifteen per cent on first plinting, First Hong Kong Serial Lights only. Also, twenty per cent of take in event of Film Lights and generous commission on possible Tom Arnold Ice Show and B.B.C.-2 ninety-eight part serial, and if B.B.C. not getting Sir Hugh Gleene to produce personally, Auntie Fu go Lediffusion, chop-chop.' She plucked the wheelbarrow from its rest. 'You find me Hong Kong Hilton, honeymoon suite,' she said, and disappeared, clopping and squeaking by turns, into the new morning.

* * *

Around her, the air-conditioner hummed, beside her the ice chinked in her mango milk shake, below her the wrinkled bay shone and twinkled, and before her, on the table, stood her typewriter, Auntie Fu selected a sheet of best-quality Hilton notepaper and fed it into the machine: slowly she typed FORTY LETTERS TO A FRIEND: THE INSIDE DOPE ON CHAIRMAN MAO. She stopped, lit a small black cheroot, and began to think.

* * *

In the executive offices of Hutchinson Publishing Group Ltd., the popping of Heidsieck corks punctuated the cheers and weeping.

'A great day, lads!' cried the Managing Director 'Who would have thought that we at Hutchinson could have followed up our staggering capture of Svetlana Salmon – '

'Stalin.'

' – thank you, Graham, Svetlana Sattin's world-shaking memoirs of her mother – '

'Father, sir.'

' – quite, followed it up, I say, by buying exclusive rights to the English version of Auntie Fu! This day will go down in the annals of money, gentlemen! Does anyone know what this book is about, by the way?'

The executives looked at one another. After a moment or two, the Head of Publicity stepped forward.

'Whatever it is,' he cried, 'it will change the course of history as we know it! It is a book no father will want his children to be without! The whole rich canvas of life unfolds as you read this timeless prose! And the first print order of two hundred thousand will retail at sixty-three bob.'

'Magnificent!' cried the Chairman. 'I can't wait to hold this matchless piece of literature in my hands and sell it!'

On the other side of London, George Weidenfeld stepped from a tenth-floor window and plummeted miserably to earth.

* * *

Moths the size of sparrows thrummed against the shutters.
A bottle of Jack Daniels Sour Mash Tennessee Whiskey
stood almost empty beside the typewriter. The waste-
basket overflowed with crumpled paper. Auntie Fu sighed,
belched, and rolled a new sheet of quarto into the machine.
MY FAMOUS NEPHEW MAO TSE-TUNG: CHAPTER
ONE, she typed. She stared at the paper. She drew the
bourbon towards her, crooning. Outside, in the corridor,
fourteen literary agents struggled noiselessly, lest genius
(or, at any rate, ten per cent of it) be disturbed. Knives
flashed in the lamplight.

*   *   *

In a small room behind a Frith Street delicatessen, two
men pored over a drawing-board, rubbing their hands.
   'What a cover!' murmured the director of Genuine
Collector's Only Paperbacks Ltd. 'What a cover! You done
a masterpiece there, Dudley, a masterpiece!'
   'Thank you,' said the art director. He ran a loving hand
over the result of minutes of concentrated effort. Beneath
the title *HEIR TO ATTILA: A TALE OF CHINESE
LUST!*, the cover portrayed a nude nymphet hanging by
her one remaining suspender over a vat of boiling sweet
and sour pork, while Mao Tse-Tung, clad only in jock-
strap and puttees, prepared to fillet her with a bloodstained bayonet. In the background, Goebbels was taking
his trousers off.
   'Thing is, Norman,' said the art director, 'How long
before we get hold of the text?'
   'Do me a favour!' said the director irritably. 'Text, text,
what's with this text business? I got a typewriter, haven't
I?'

*   *   *

From beneath a mountain of wastepaper and old bottles,
Auntie Fu watched with tiny glittering eyes as a row of
agents pleaded with her from the bed.
   'I have sold the English edition to Hutchinson,' keened
the first agent.

'I have sold the translation rights in the proposed Greek edition to Collins,' moaned the second.

'I have sold the rights of the proposed Bantu translation of the Welsh translation of the Norse to MacMillan,' wailed the third.

'Just tell us, Autie Fu!' cried the fourth, 'when are you going to write something?'

A hiccup shook the heap of rubbish. They heard the noise of ratchets, the sound of keys striking erratically home.

BOOK ABOUT MAO TSE-TUNG wrote Auntie Fu.

* * *

High above Ludgate Circus, the editor of *The Observer* handed round a packet of Weights, and his staff fell fawning to their knees.

'Go on, lads, take them!' cried the editor. 'You've earned them. What a coup, snatching the serial rights to the Esperanto edition from under Thompson's very nose, and for a mere eighty thousand, at that! And all the *Sunday Telegraph*'s got is Bertrand Russell's account of how his son almost met Chiang Kai-Shek! Tell me, what layout plans do we have?'

'Well,' said the art editor, 'we thought we'd blow up some lovely big snaps of Chinamen in deckchairs, all sort of, you know, grainy, so's no one could recognise them – '

'*Fabulous!*' squealed his nine assistants.

' – and then, you know, tons of sort of mock-Chinoiserie writing for the headlines and cross heads – '

'*Super!*' shrieked his staff.

' – and then have the text running right to left so's you can only read it by, you know, holding it upside down in a mirror. A sort of, well, you know, *happening!*'

'*Swinging!*' screamed the assistants, grasping one another's mini-smocks, and watching the editor carefully.

'I like it,' said the editor. 'I like it very much. I mean, it will really *look* like literature, right?' He glanced suddenly at his watch. 'I wish to God the stuff would get here, though.'

* * *

The agents, because there was no more space for them among six months' effluvia, had moved into the bathroom, and sat gloomily round the lilac bidet, playing gin rummy and growing beards. Somewhere beneath the mouldering trash next door, Auntie Fu crouched staring at the line she had written on her last sheet of notepaper, two weeks before. The line read: THE YELLOW PERIL: AN AUNTIE REMEMBERS. But, try as she might, Auntie Fu found that she could not remember anything at all.

A Scandal in Manchuria

'Secret agents in China's security police were told to model their activities on Sherlock Holmes, it was learned in Hong Kong today.'

Daily Express

I find it recorded in my notebook that it was a bleak and windy day towards the end of September. It being the anniversary of the Glorious People's Revolution, I had called upon my illustrious friend with the intention of wishing him the compliments of the season. You may imagine my astonishment when, having been admitted to his rooms by Mrs. Hud Son, I found therein not their regular occupant but an individual with a narrow, somewhat cadaverous face, an aquiline nose, a high forehead, and fine, arched eyebrows beneath which burned a pair of deep-sunken grey eyes of particular intensity. Though long absence on the Afghan frontier had, on several occasions, proved to have introduced unfortunate gaps into my reminiscence, it was nevertheless impossible for me to fail to recognise the features of Mr Basil Rathbone. He was lounging in the fireplace, smoking a grey woollen dressing-gown and attempting to inscribe the name of Mao Tse-Tung on the sofa with a Rivyakin machine-pistol, with little success. Most of the sideboard lay in ruins, amid an agglomeration of shattered test-tubes, riddled cheroot-boxes, fragments of cold grouse foo yong, the remains of a microscope, and half a gasogene.

'Perhaps, esteemed visitor,' I murmured, bowing low after the manner of ex-medical officers of the 17th/21st Hangchow Foot, 'you will be glacious enough to bestow on this humble servant the leasons for your plesence here in the chambers of the world's gleatest detective?'

The queer visitor laid his pistol aside, and allowed himself a laugh which can only be described as indescribable. I was beginning to regret my lack of foresight in leaving my service revolver in my other smock; despite its lack of foresight, it is a formidable weapon at close quarters, if you have any. But hardly had I taken my first cautionary step towards the figure in the grate than he sprang up with the agility of an ox, passed a hand across his face, and revealed the familiar omelette complexion and tiny prune-stone eyes of the greatest detective whom it has ever been my good fortune to batten on for a living.

'Ah, so!' I exclaimed.

'Plecisely, mly dear Wat Sun. I tlust you will forgive this little deception of mine which allows me to pass among the milling hordes of Peking, entirely noticed.'

'My dear friend!' I cried.

Holmes smiled tolerantly, and, taking down his old Stradivarius, began stuffing it with Persian slippers which he kept for the purpose in a jar of Black Navy Shag.

'How often have I said to you,' he murmured, 'that when you have discovered the tluth, whatever lemains, *however implobable*, must be impossible?'

'Wonderful!' I ejaculated.

'Commonplace,' said Holmes. He drew a telegram from his left sleeve. 'What do you make of this dog, Wat Sun? Is it not curious?'

'But it's not a dog!' I cried.

'That is what is curious,' remarked Holmes.

I perused the script.

'Happy Anniversary,' I read, 'May All Your Tloubles Be Little Ones.'

Holmes puffed at his violin.

'A damned funny thing for a dog to say, eh?' he said. Outside the window of 221B, a rickshaw wheel scraped along the kerb. My friend started up. 'But here, unless I am mistaken, is our client!'

I ran to the curtain, just in time to see the familiar figure of the milkman disappearing beneath the austere portals of 219A with two cartons of yoghurt and a gill of double cream.

'You are mistaken,' I said.

'Ah, so,' replied Holmes. 'Well, nobody's perfect. Wat sun. I myself have failed to compile several monoglaphs on the subject. Tell me, how did you allive at your conclusion?'

'You know my methods, Holmes.'

'Excellent!' he cried.

'Elementaly,' said I.

It was during this discourse that I perceived the fine-drawn features of my friend becoming perturbed.

'There is something ladically long,' he said at last. 'But I am unable to put finger on it.'

Springing to his feet, he stepped nimbly to the vast library beneath which his bookshelves groaned, and withdrew therefrom a slim text which I recognised as *The Glorious Security Forces Manual Of Police Procedure*. Thumbing the pages rapidly, Holmes lit upon a passage, and frowned over it for some time. Finally, he looked up, the noble countenance clear.

'You have been speaking wrong lines!' he exclaimed.

'Excellent!' I cried.

'Elementaly,' said he.

We might have proceeded in this vein far into the night, had not that instant brought to our door a thunderous knocking fit to let loose all the demons of Hades.

'Who can it be?' I whispered.

'Charles Augustus Milverton,' said Holmes, rapidly preparing a little wall-poster on the ashes of one hundred and forty different varieties of pipe, cigar, cigarette, and violin tobacco. 'The worst man in Peking. You have your old service revolver, Wat Sun?'

'No.'

'Plaise be for that!' cried Holmes. 'I have only just lecovered flom hole in foot leceived in our last little enterplise!'*

Saying which, he flung open the door. Immediately, a small bearded man strode into the room. Holmes grasped him by the lapels.

'Plofessor Molly Arty!' he roared. 'The Napoleon of clime!'

*The Musglave Litual. A story for which the world is not yet plepared.

138

Our visitor shook himself free of Holmes's iron clasp, and glared at us in what appeared to be some puzzlement. Beneath his arm he bore a number of small red books.

'Eening thoughts!' he bellowed. 'Gitchore eening thoughts ere! See wot Chairman Mao thinks abart the Ound of the Baskervilles! All the closing city thoughts! Gitchore eening thoughts!'

Holmes advanced upon the fellow with a sturdy poker, his eyes gleaming with discovery.

'See, Wat Sun!' he cried. 'Do you not mark that the fellow's beard is that of a much smaller man with a limp and a pliceless collection of Ludy Vallee lecords?'

'Of course!' I replied, leaping upon the forged news-vendor and seizing the growth upon his chin. 'Come out flom behind there, Eileen Adler! To Sher Lok Holmes you are always *the* woman!'

'LUBBISH!' shrieked Holmes, wrenching my quarry from me. 'Smell his ears! He are lecently taking his Ph.D. flom Uppsala!'

With an oath, he cast the fellow aside and grasped me by the sleeve, dragging me out of the door.

'I play God we are not too late!' he cried, hailing a rickshaw. 'These are much deeper waters than I had thought, and may even involve the Giant Lat of Sumatra!'

As the 3.15 pulled slowly out of Peking Central, I leaned across to my companion. Something had been troubling me.

'Excuse, please, Holmes,' I said. 'But he have been our newsvendor for thirty-thlee years.'

A rare smile flickered across my friend's lips as he lit his favourite magnifying-glass.

'It has long been an axiom of mine that the little things are infinitely the most important,' he said.

As the suburbs of the city fell away behind us, Holmes excused himself and left the compartment; when he returned, he took his seat opposite me, a quizzical expression on his face. He was silent for some time. Finally, he leaned forward and said:

'I tlust, sir, you will spend an enjoyable evening in Tientsin.'

I stared at him. He allowed himself a polite laugh.

'You see, my dear sir,' he said, 'it is not at all difficult to constluct a series of infelences, each dependant upon its pledecessor and each simple in itself. If, after doing so, one simply knocks out the central infelences and plesents one's audience with the starting-point and the conclusion, one may ploduce a startling, though possibly a meletlicious, effect. Now since this tlain is bound for Tientsin, and since you are on it, and since it is getting dark, I merely applied the plocess of deduction.'

I cleared my throat.

'It are I, Holmes,' I remarked. 'Wat Sun.'

He started.

'Good God!' he cried. 'You have lemoved your hat! I did not lecognise you.'

He thereupon fell into a deep reverie, from which he did not emerge until our train puffed into the desolate station of Tientsin. As we hurried along the platform, my companion stopped suddenly, and, bending, began examining a number of objects through his meerschaum. He straightened triumphantly.

'A severed thumb, a golden pince-nez, a beryl colonet, and five ollange pips!' he exclaimed. 'Flom which we may deduce that a short-sighted gleenglocer of noble birth has lecently jumped flom his tlain in such haste as to shut his left hand in the door! We are close upon our qually, Wat Sun!'

It is with a heavy heart that I take up my pen to write these the last words in which I shall ever record the singular gifts by which my friend Mr. Sher Lok Holmes was distinguished. All that night we travelled by dog-cart through the drear landscape, north through Changchun, and into the inimical Manchurian wastes, until we arrived finally at that dreadful spot on the Sungari where the boiling waters plunge over that teetering precipice into the raging torrent below. It was here that my old friend, a weird light in his eyes, at last got down, before a narrow gate that barred the only access to the river, guarded by two men who menaced us as we approached.

'No ently!' cried the taller of the two. 'The dless lehearsal for Glorious Annual Swim of Glorious Leader now taking place.'

140

With a flourish, Holmes produced his card, and the regular police officers fell back deferentially to open the gate; we strode rapidly through, and up the winding path towards the river bank. A few minutes brought us to a small opening where, to my utter astonishment two men were inflating the water wings of a familiar figure, and preparing to lower him into the water. Holmes put out a hand.

'Stay, Wat Sun!' he hissed. 'I would not lisk the life of my oldest fliend. God, the devilish cunning of the man. Thank God we are in time!'

'But Holmes!' I cried, 'Do you not lecognise . . . '

It was too late. Flinging back his Inverness cape, my companion sprang from the bushes and, under the startled eyes of the retainers, fixed his steely hands about the adipose neck of the figure in the bathing costume.

'So, Molly Arty, we meet at last!' bellowed Holmes, and, dragging his quarry to the very edge, applied to his limbs one of those dread ju-jitsu holds he had so often described to me. But the other immediately shook himself free, grasped Holmes's nose between thumb and forefinger, and before I could unfreeze my petrified limbs, shoved into that dreadful cauldron of swirling water and seething foam the foremost champion of the law of his generation. As the beloved deer-stalker sank for the third time, the two retainers rushed forward and began to cheer.

'Long live Chairman Mao!'

'So pellish all assassins!'

'Death to the enemies of Chairman Mao!'

'Chairman Mao will live for a thousand years!'

I deliberated briefly as to the most expeditious course of action, and decided at last to withdraw into the shrubbery until nightfall. Of the calumny which was subsequently heaped upon my unfortunate friend, I need not speak; only now, from the sanctuary of the *Observer Colour Supplement* contracts office, am I grateful for the opportunity to clear his memory of the attacks upon him whom I shall ever regard as the best and wisest man whom I have ever known.

And Is There Sturgeon
Still For Tea?

Gordon Lonsdale, the Russian spy, was recently asked in East Berlin what his plans for the future were, now his professional career had ended. 'I want to make a lot of money out of my memoirs,' he said, 'and lead the life of an English country gentleman.'

The Observer

Andrei Andreyovich shuffled dispiritedly into the master bedroom and tugged at the curtain cords. Watery sunlight filtered through the cardboard mullions, and as it fell across a slim figure huddled in the fourposter bed, the sleeper stirred.

'Is not exactly top-hole morning, tovarich,' said the valet. 'Is very likely coming down cats and dogs before long, or I'm a Dutchman. Gorblimey, yes.'

The master raised himself on one elbow and stared gloomily at his man.

'I wish to hell you'd remember not to call me tovarich,' he said.

'Apologies, Gordon Gordonovich, but is not easy for ex-glorious peoples' carburettor operative to say 'sir' and wipe away forty years of bleeding democracy.'

Beneath the mound of bedclothes, Gordon Gordonovich clenched a small, manicured fist.

'You're a gentleman's gentleman now, Andrei Andreyovich,' he said.

The valet stared out over the leaden steppes with a terrible sigh.

'Is nothing lower in world,' he muttered. 'I am capitalist

142

lackey, Gordon Gordonovich, sir. A lickspittle. Have sold out glorious democratic birthright for lousy lucre accumulated without sweat of brow, shiver me timbers.'

'It was a damned good book,' shouted Gordon Gordonovich.

'Begging your pardon, sir, is load of old cobblers from start to finish,' said the valet meekly. 'Is rubbishy deviationist tract from imperialist cultural depredation, look you.'

Lonsdale pulled himself into a sitting position.

'Where's the mail?' he said.

Andrei Andreyovich shrugged, and his enormous frock-coat shook dust into the pale sunbeams.

'Is not come,' he said. He turned back to the window. 'Ah. Is coming up hill from village now, wouldn't you know it? Yes, it is Mr Nobbs the postman. He is carrying a sack. What has he got in the sack? He has got letters for Mummy in the sack. He has got a packet for Daddy in the sack. What has he got in his hand? He has got . . . '

Lonsdale screamed. A biscuit-tin lid bearing a view of Kenilworth Castle fell off its nail and rolled erratically across the buckled linoleum. The valet frowned.

'Is anything wrong, Gordon Gordonovich, sir?'

'Mr. Nobbs,' muttered Lonsdale weakly, 'What's all that muck about Mr Nobbs?'

The valet pulled out a dog-eared paperback and flourished it.

'Is top-hole Colloquial English Part II Advanced Students, old fruit,' he said. 'Is chapter called *Hallo, Postman.*'

Lonsdale sank back slowly, and closed his eyes.

'Just go and get the mail, Andrei Andreyovich, there's a good lad.'

The servant shambled out, and Lonsdale, sighing, stood up. He wore a pair of very old, very threadbare silk pyjamas, and a faded M.C.C. cravat, and, as he moved painfully across the icy floor, he seemed to be aging with every step. Lovingly, he took a gramophone record from a rusty meat-safe, and put it on. *We'll Gather Lilacs* wheezed across the room, and his eyes filled with small, bright tears. *My Life As A Masterspy For The Glorious*

143

Peoples' Republic had sold thirty-one copies; he needed riding-boots, tattersall waistcoats, decanters, family portraits, persian rugs, George IV teaspoons – but the dream was fading, fading. A knock at the door rattled through his meditation. Andrei Andreyovich mooched back in.

'I say, I say, I say,' he said.

'Well?'

'It is forty minutes past nine and all is well, my old darling,' said the valet, bowing deferentially. 'Here is mail.'

Lonsdale fell on the pile of parcels, tearing off the wrappings, and hurling them aside. Among other things was a cardboard box, full of tufts of hair, attached to rubber bands. He took one out and adjusted it around the valet's head.

'It's a forelock,' he said. 'You touch it when you see me coming, understand? The rest are for distribution among the villagers.' He laid the other articles out on the bed, tenderly. There were forty bound volumes of *Country Life*, a shooting-stick, a Collins's Gentleman's Diary, an Inverness cape, a red plastic carnation, a tin of trout flies, four pewter tankards, a Rolls-Royce radiator grill, three pairs of Hush Puppies, a satin eye-patch, two pairs of plusfours, a carefully battered gold Hunter, a barometer, a stuffed ferret, six Old Harrovian ties, and an oar.

'Not bad for a start,' said Lonsdale. He slipped into a pair of plusfours, knotted a tie loosely about his neck, and tapped the barometer three or four times with the ferret. Then he handed the radiator to his servant.

'Take this down to Igor,' he said, he'll know what to do with it.'

Ten minutes later, the servant came back. Behind him stood a tiny man, in a baggy morning suit. His feet were bare, and half his face was hidden under a mildewed bowler hat. Lonsdale stared at him.

'Is my brother-in-law, Lavrenti,' explained Andrei Andreyovich with a smile. 'Is applying for vacancy as butler.'

'Has he any experience?'

'Is master of colloquial English,' said the valet. 'Is first-class spot-on butler, blow me down.'

144

He nudged the dwarf with the oar.

'Yes, it is Mr. Nobbs the postman,' said the dwarf. 'He is carrying a sack. He is carrying a sack. He is carrying a . . .'

He lapsed into silence.

'I coach him special,' said Andrei Andreyovich proudly. 'Also has special talent for butlering. Listen.'

He jabbed at the midget once more.

'The problem seems to be a fairly straightforward one, sir,' said the midget, in a thick Ukrainian accent, 'If I might offer my advice, I would suggest that you terminate your engagement to the niece of Lord Blanding's rich Argentinian third cousin, thereby enabling Mr. Fink-Nottle to liquidate his stock in the company of Lady Clitterwick's long-lost brother Wilfred who will then feel himself free to return the replica of the pearl necklace inadvertently stolen from the cabin of Catsmeat Potter-Purbright's ex-fiancee . . .'

Lonsdale leapt forward suddenly, grasped the midget by the scruff of the neck, and hurled him down the stairs.

'Is great problem getting domestic staff these days, what?' said Andrei Andreyovich brightly. He reached for his forelock, which was now hanging under his left ear, and tugged it dutifully. His master looked at him for a long time. Finally he said:

'What's today's schedule?'

'Is opening of fox-hunting season,' read Andrei Andreyovich from his cuff. 'Is meeting pack in forecourt of Red Lion at eleven sharp.'

He went behind a screen and re-emerged with a bundle of clothes which he threw on the floor. Lonsdale dressed slowly in front of the yellowed pier-glass, and while he knotted the string around his corduroy breeches and pinned up his patched battledress blouse, he dreamed of immaculate pinks, and gleaming boots, and captivated debutantes, and prancing hunters, and grovelling villagers. Because that was all he had ever asked of life back home, and when they hadn't given it to him, he had tried, in his small, brave way, to destroy them. They had had it coming to them, he reflected. I hope they know how spies are born.

'Is time,' said his valet. 'Igor is bringing Rolls round to door.'

They clattered down the peeling staircase together, and through the bare echoing hall, and out into the yard. Igor, the chauffeur, stood among the puddles, between the shafts of the dog-cart; he wore an old navy cap, and stood gazing levelly into the distance, with the Rolls-Royce radiator hanging from his neck by a piece of string. Master and servant climbed aboard the cart, and it creaked off. A crowd of small boys followed it for a little way, throwing rocks and shouting popular local obscenities. A mile up the rutted road, they stopped at a scrofulous hut; a crowd of six or seven elderly residents, who had been sitting beneath an inn-sign which read 'The Red Lion' (upside down), stood up, took off their forelocks, and waved them feebly. There was a small cheer as Lonsdale dismounted, and one or two of the villagers shouted 'By Jove!' and 'Hallo Mister Nobbs!' and 'God Save The King!'

'Is good crowd, no?' whispered Andrei Andreyovich.

'Was demanding three roubles a head, but I tell them two, and not a penny more, heh-heh.'

Lonsdale smiled limply at his serfs, and went inside the hut. The walls were plastered with old beer-mats, and behind a trestle-table, which supported a dented samovar, stood a little fat man in an apron.

'Good morrow, mine host,' cried Lonsdale.

The landlord drew a pint of cold tea, and handed it across the table.

'Gorblimey,' he murmured. This done, he took off his apron, picked up his wheeltapper's hammer, and vanished through a hole in the wall.

Lonsdale poured the tea onto the floor, and went outside again. Igor had brought up an old carthorse, which had gone to sleep, and Andrei Andreyovich held the leads of a pair of dogs, both of which had only one eye and were dribbling vacantly. He smiled encouragingly at Lonsdale, who licked his lips, and got up on the carthorse.

'Right,' he said, and with his free hand, the valet drew a mangy cat from his breast pocket and threw it into the road, at the same time releasing the dogs. The cat shrieked, once and shinned up a nearby tree. The one-eyed dogs

146

hesitated for a moment, then began to limp off aimlessly in opposite directions. The carthorse failed to wake up. After about five minutes, Lonsdale got down. Andrei Andreyovich shuffled up to him.

'We go play polo now, my old mate?'

Lonsdale shook his head.

'We open bazaar? We shoot grouses? We visit Junior Carlton, yes?'

'Not today,' said Gordon Gordonovich. And he began to walk away, across the fields, looking at the ground. The peasants stared after him, until he was no more than an ambling speck, and then, as one man, they turned to Andrei Andreyovich.

'Is pretty top-hole life being country gentleman, no?' said one.

Andrei Andreyovich picked up a stone, and shied it at the cat.

'I should cocoa,' he said.

Kremlin Blues

In the small, grey-painted kitchen of their pokey two-roomed flat Leonid Brezhnev stared across the bare boards of the breakfast table at Alexei Nikolayevich Kosygin.

'Well?' he said.

Alexei Nikolayevich raised heavy, red-rimmed eyes.

'Well what?' he said.

'Well smile sometimes, that's what,' said Brezhnev irritably. 'Smile like you did for the fatfaced British industrialists! For them you had plenty of lousy grinning, for me nothing. Eight days you've been home Alexei Nikolayevich, and I didn't hear a kind word yet. What am I, some kind of a nothing, you should treat me this way?'

Kosygin did not reply. Instead, he pushed his coffeecup aside, and groaned, very softly.

'So what's wrong with the coffee?' said Brezhnev. 'I made it the way you like it, didn't I? It's got real beans in it, Alexei.'

'In England,' said Kosygin quietly, 'it comes like powder. A brown powder. You just add hot water, and you know what happens?'

'So surprise me.'

'Flavour buds burst, that's what happens,' said Kosygin. His eyes misted reminiscently. 'They tell you all about it on these big wall-posters they got. And *such* coffee, Leonid! Like before the Revolution.'

Brezhnev thrust a knuckle into his gasp to stifle it.

'What's the matter with you, Alexei Nikolayevich, you some kind of a nut or something? The neighbours hear you talk that way, it's curtains, believe me.'

148

Kosygin shrugged moodily, and his sad eyes travelled slowly about the tiny room, wincing as they took in the cracked lino, and the peeling paint, and the lithographs of Lenin on the unlovely walls.

'What we need,' he said, 'is a bit of cretonne. Something with colour in it. Regency stripe maybe, with a dark ceiling to set it off. Dignity, a bit of class. Maybe a stainless steel draining board, and some nice blue china, and a few of those tea-towels, they got pictures of Cilla Black on them. In England, Leonid, they have these yellow plastic chairs and Formica tables, all you do is wipe them down with a moist rag, beautiful. And carpets, like in the best cinemas. Oy, Leonid, such furniture they got in Selfridge's!'

Brezhnev glared bitterly at his flat-mate from hurt, narrowed eyes.

'England, England, England, that's all I hear!' he cried. 'You think we didn't see those pictures of you mooching about Regent Street or wherever it is, with your face breathing up the lousy windows? I tell you, a pretty rotten impression it created over here, a Number One Soviet citizen standing in front of a load of non-stick frying-pans with his eyes sticking out like organ stops.' He stared down at his clenched fists, and opened them tremblingly. 'You think *I* couldn't do with a bit of Pink Camay now and then, or some of that washing powder, it keeps your hands soft like a baby's? Look at these red patches, Alexei Nikolayevich, from lousy Gum soda! I wouldn't care, it don't even get the rotten plates clean. But do *I* nag all the time?'

But Kosygin had closed his eyes, and a small smile edged his lips.

'At the Palace, the Queen and I –'

'Name dropper.'

' – the Queen and I ate off these gold plates they got. With genuine gold cutlery, yet. And you know what we ate?'

'I should know what debauched tyrants stuff themselves with?'

'Oysters we ate, and little ducks the size of sparrows, and beef, it melted in your mouth like butter. That's what we ate.'

Brezhnev snorted.

'No wonder you sicked up the borsch last night. The first time in five years you bring up my cooking.' He blew his nose suddenly on a tattered rag. 'Two hours I queued for those beetroots, Alexei Nikolayevich.'

Kosygin stood up, pushed back his chair, and walked slowly to the window. In the street below, dark lumps of citizenry struggled against the February blizzard; icy wind clattered the little windows; a bird landed on the sill, peered at him, and died.

'They took me home from the Palace in a Rolls-Royce,' he murmured. 'You ever been in a Rolls-Royce, Leonid?'

'Do me a favour.'

'Thick beige carpet, it comes right up to the welts of your boots. Genuine hide upholstery. Little individual walnut tables, you pull them out and put your drinks on them. You want the windows open, you press a little button, they go down. Fantastic!'

'I don't want to know,' said Brezhnev sullenly. 'Don't tell me. It's still three weeks before my next go on the Praesidium tricycle. Don't talk to me from Rolls-Royces.'

'And in Claridges,' said Kosygin, hearing nothing but his memory, 'you ring a bell, they bring you Tizer in the middle of the night. Leave your shoes out, they clean them. You want TV, they bring you TV. With three channels, yet. And such cleaning and pressing, a same-day service like you never seen.'

'That's right,' said Brezhnev darkly. 'I never seen.'

Kosygin turned around to face him.

'You know something, Leonid? We ought to get an au pair.'

'A what?'

'An au pair. In England, you haven't got an au pair, you're nobody. A Swiss girl maybe, young, who can make baked apple, and do the beds, and yodel a bit. Take some of the work off your hands, Leonid, an au pair. All you have to do is talk Russian to them and teach them to frug and which buses to catch down Nevski Prospekt, and for forty roubles a month, you got an au pair.'

'Us? A *servant*?'

'So who else should have one if not us? The two most

powerful men in the world and we still have to draw lots for who drags the lousy coal up four flights of stairs? I'll put an advert in the paper.'

'Sure. You do that. And maybe when we're in Siberia, she can carry the shovels for us.'

'You worry too much, Leonid,' said Kosygin. He grasped his flatmate's shoulder passionately. 'Don't you want to live a little?'

'No. Personally, Alexei Nikolayevich, I want to live a lot. You put that advertisement in the paper, and I give us about ten minutes, at the outside.'

'Pah! I tell you what, tovarich, I shall get into my swinging gear, and together we shall go down to the *Pravda* small-ads department, and . . .'

'Your swinging which?'

'Wait!' cried Kosygin, and was gone. For some minutes, a noise of zips and buckles and heavy breathing shook the flimsy building, while Brezhnev hovered nervously by the sink, wringing his hands and listening for steps upon the stair, until, suddenly, Kosygin leapt back into the kitchen. Brezhnev reeled. The Chairman of the Council of Ministers beamed beneath a green suede Donovan cap. His bulky torso strained at the buttons of a mauve corduroy blazer, down the front of which a wide luminous tie hung from a polka-dotted collar, reaching almost to the knees of a pair of primrose bell-bottom trousers. Alexei Nikolayevich beamed.

'I am swinging, yes?' he cried.

Brezhnev's face was the colour of rancid curds.

'Not yet,' he croaked. 'But soon, Alexei Nikolayevich, soon.'

Kosygin stroked his jacket lovingly.

'Like Prince Tony Jones,' he murmured, enrapt. 'Posh, Classy.'

'What you got in that box?' said Brezhnev hoarsely.

Kosygin blushed. Slowly, shyly, he lifted the cardboard lid. And took out a crown.

'Not real stones, you understand,' he said to the goggling Brezhnev. 'Paste. I had it made special. Like a glove it fits.'

Slowly, his colleague stretched out a hand to touch the dread jewellery. Brighter than the gems, glittered his eyes.

'Excuse me a moment, Alexei Nikolayevich,' he murmured, in a strange, far voice. 'I think I hear the cat.'

In the dark corridor, Leonid Brezhnev lifted the ancient receiver, and dialled a number, carefully. Within five minutes, two M.V.D. men had come and gone, carrying between them a bizarre, shrieking figure in an op-art cloak and busby. From the window of his bedroom. Brezhnev watched the weird trio struggle through the snow. Then he drew the curtains, pulled an eiderdown about his shoulders and, seating himself before the mirror and opening the cardboard box, he placed upon his head a very good likeness of the Imperial State Crown of England.

He sat there, motionless and strangely smiling, until all light had faded from the sky.

*Towards the
Four-Minute Heart*

'*There is an obvious danger in the general pattern: this is that
doctors may become infected by a spirit of international competition – a kind of rivalry in medical athletics.*'
The Observer

Grey sleet swirled up Southampton Water on a Force Ten
gale, lashing the pitiful queue of emaciated shapes waiting
to board the *S.S. United States*. From behind the plate-
glass windows of the customs hall, British heart-teams
peered through binoculars, waiting for deaths. Veins beat
in their temples as, from time to time, a weightless em-
barkee would rebel before a sudden gust, fall, and be blown
about the quay, then, infuriatingly, struggle to his meagre
feet again, inadequately aided by the twiggy arm of a fellow
emigrant.

'God knows what keeps the so-and-so's alive!' shrieked a
senior cardiac consultant, who had for days past been
cheated of his quarry. 'Why can't they peg out on British
soil like gentlemen? Where's their bloody patriotism?'

'If only we had the money,' moaned a bag-eyed con-
frere, honing his scalpel longingly against a sterilised palm.
'In my opinion, America should be banned from all international transplant competition! What chance do we stand
against Donor Scholarships, lads? It's against the whole
spirit of the game. It's sheer professionalism, that's what it
is! Why, only last week the University of Minnesota Medical School endowed a further fifty thousand dollars in
bursaries. A potential donor I'd had my eye on for
months...'

153

'. . . not 45-year-old father of six lapsed Roman Catholic unemployed dishwasher Gerald O'Shaughnessy whose brain was irreparably damaged in a drinking accident?'

'The very same. He's been taken on by Harvard as a nuclear physicist on a five-thousand-dollar Donor Scholarship. Poor sod won't even get the chance to open his new pencil-box before he snuffs it, and they'll have that heart of his out before he even hits the ground.'

Registrars keened strategically, dreaming of promotion.

'It's making a mockery of the amateur status of the British donor!' cried a surgeon. 'Where will it end?'

Outside, the Yale band struck up *Abide With Me*, and, as pom-pom girls danced shrilly on the bridge, the migrating donors shuffled erratically up the gangplank to where slavering men in long white coats waited hungrily to drag them aboard.

Sirens wailed. Hawsers clattered on the dock. Slowly, tugs drew the great ship towards open water. And, as night came down, in the specially appointed cabins a hundred ophthalmoscopes winked on.

* * *

In the New York headquarters of the World Health Organisation, the delegate from Tanzania leapt passionately to his feet.

'Mr President!' he cried. 'May I on behalf of my country strongly protest at the proposed international ratification of the latest South African heart transplant and the six-month survival of the so-called patient as a, and I quote, "record"?'

'Hear, hear!' yelled back the Asian bloc, beating their desks.

'While,' continued the Tanzanian delegate, 'the white fascist minority continues its crimes in South Africa, I put it to the assembly that we do not recognise the validity of all such operations, and ban South Africa from international medical competition.'

Amid shrieks, and a hail of ornamental inkstands (both for and against the motion), the President rose.

'I should like to point out, gentlemen,' he said wearily,

'that, insofar as the heart of a black man has already been sewn into the body of a white man by South African surgeons, the country has already gone a long way towards meeting...'

The President disappeared in a maelstrom of fists, boots, and diplomatic bags, which, when it subsided, revealed that the Presidency was now vacant. The body, still twitching faintly, was carried into the corridor, where, following a brief, vicious tug-o'war, it was won by a team of Algerian surgeons, who bore it swiftly towards the gents'.

*   *   *

'And here at the East London Heart Hospital, we welcome listeners back after the Tea Interval with the news that there's going to be a change of surgeons at the feet end. I think it's going to be – is that Sir Nigel Bryce-Gorringe, Freddie?'

'I think so, John, though it's not too easy to tell behind the mask, but from that characteristic flip of his cuff as he turns and comes in, I'd say it almost certainly was. We've seen a great start from Professors Berk and Hare, who have of course opened for England on many occasions, and it'll be interesting to see how Bryce-Gorringe follows it up. Won't it, Norman?'

'Yes indeed, Freddie. It looks to me like a typical Bryce-Gorringe field placing, with three registrars strung out down the leg side, a theatre sister just square of point, and two housemen close in at mid-on, an attacking field, certainly, and – oh, my goodness, what a glorious late-cut!'

'Incomparable, Norman, a splendid. wristy stroke, listeners, just fine of the left atrium, and it's going deep, between first and second pulmonary veins, past the semilunar valve, and I don't think they're going to stop it –'

'No, John, that's going all the way. It's amazing what these chaps can do when they get a bit of arc-light on their backs. I think this afternoon's play will give the South African team something to think about, don't you? And now, till close of play, I'm handing the commentary over to...'

*   *   *

At Reykjavik Airport, sixteen members of the Rhodesian transplant team, heavily disguised behind long black beards and false noses, stepped warily down from their Dakota and peered nervously into the sleet.

After them came a line of native bearers, carrying on their heads two deep-frozen figures, a heart-lung machine, an electro-encephalograph and several crates of instruments. To them, similarly disguised, entered the scurrying figure of the Governor of the local hospital. He grasped the senior consultant's hand, and shook it warmly.

'An honour, gentleman,' he wept, 'a very great honour! To think that in my little infirmary your great team will at last perform.'

But, alas, it was not to be. At that moment, around the corner of the baggage shed, galloped a long screaming line of third-year seismology students, shouting Icelandic obscenities and waving banners bearing such legends as 'Eff Off Rhodesians!' and 'Nazi Hart Players Go Hoam!'

As one man, the surgeons and their staff turned and sprinted for their plane, whose pilot, from long experience, had turned it into the wind and kept the revs up. The door slammed, the engines howled, and the battered aircraft lurched forward down the frozen runway, and took off.

It was the twelfth time that week.

* * *

Down the long, wavering line of raw recruits, Lieut. Colonel Andrei Andreyevich marched, stopping here and there to tap a button or pull down a battle-tunic. Any soldier remaining on his feet after such assaults was immediately put under close arrest and transferred to the Mongolian frontier divisions.

'Men!' roared Andrei Andreyevich. 'Welcome to the 17th/21st Kaganov Malingerers! Stand easy!'

They did so, whereupon four of their number, for whom the effort was too much, sank to their knees and expired. Snowflakes whispered over them.

'Headstrong fools!' cried Andrei Andreyevich, with such force that those of his men who were not yet deaf immediately became so. 'Let them be the last of this gallant band to die with their boots on! I would remind you, comrades, that ours is a special brigade. Only those volunteers feeble enough to have failed the medical have been allowed to join!'

A nonagenarian from Tomsk cheered weedily and died.

'As you men know, the great and glorious Red Army has always provided the backbone of the international teams that have carried our motherland to the forefront of the competitive – you should pardon the expression – world. Today, it is your turn to be that backbone, or, rather, heh-heh-heh, that liver, that heart, those shimmering lights. For to us it has fallen to be the world's first Transplant Relay Team!'

He paused dramatically, and a keen decimating wind whistled through the assembled skeletonry.

'You will be grouped into teams of four, for example, Gonchov, Kalinovich, Rivski and Lebnev. At the given signal, our glorious people's surgeons will attempt to put Gonchov's heart into Kalinovich, Kalinovich's into Rivski, Rivski's into Lebnev, and Lebnev's into Gonchov again. You will be expected to remain formally alive for at least a week afterwards, and God help any man I catch dying!'

The colonel turned, and his men – with the exception of those who had made the mistake of trying to return his salute – crept happily behind him towards the row of labs.

*　　*　　*

And five thousand miles due south, in the fetid equatorial gloom, two naked men sat in a tiny clearing, surrounded by the remains of several others. The Chief looked up sadly at his Witch Doctor.

'Well, Doc, that the last of the tribe,' he murmured.

'Looks like it,' said the Witch Doctor.

'Funny thing,' said the Chief, 'what happened to all those stories of great natural athletes coming out of the bush and carrying off all the medals and everything?'

The Witch Doctor shrugged.

'Considering the shortage of coaching,' he said, 'we done pretty good. Old Ngaga Mbobe had seven lungs in him before he finally snuffed it, and Uncle Bim was so full of kidneys, I had to stitch his liver onto his left elbow.'

The Chief stared gloomily at a pile of organs.

'One thing's certain, doc,' he said. 'We sure as hell ain't ready for the Olympics.'

'Who cares?' said the Witch Doctor. 'You know what they say.'

'What's that?'

The Witch Doctor smiled behind his mask.

'The object is not to win,' he said, 'but to take part.'

The Animals Went In
Two by Two

'According to the October issue of Science Journal, *intelligent animals will be bred for low-grade labour by 2025 AD.'*
The Guardian

In a bruise-coloured Ilford evening, Henry Mooncroft crunched miserably up the gravelled path of Dunspendin, gloom nagging at his every cell.

It had been a vile day at the office.

At 11 a.m., Osric, the new office dog, had put three lumps of sugar in Mooncroft's tea and, upon gentle reprimand, had sunk its fangs into his calf. At 12.30, the horse that delivered the mid-day papers had trodden Mooncroft's wastebasket to slivers, and in lieu of apology had eaten the cucumber sandwiches to which he had been looking forward all morning. Not that he was a particular fan of cucumber sandwiches, but it was one of the few comestibles that did not bring the animal staff out on strike. By nature, Mooncroft was a ham-and-chutney addict, but the arrival of a large belligerent sow in the packing department had spelt the end of all such offensive goodies. (Indeed, a few days before, he had consumed a surreptitious sausage in the saloon bar of The Grapes, only to be instantly reported by a red setter who had been enjoying a quiet pint in the public and noticed Mooncroft's indiscretion. The unfortunate biped had returned to his desk to find a thickset mandrill, who had been elected shop-steward, stamping on his dictaphone; it refused to go away until Mooncroft had delivered a written apology.)

After lunch, spent wretched and cucumberless in St.

James's Park where he had been cautioned for loitering by a swan, Mooncroft had had to sign an office memorandum agreeing to take no further action against the mice with which his somewhat elderly office was overrun; this followed a complaint made by the office cats (who came in part-time to lick stamps) that the mice were traditional fringe-benefits: any attempt to exterminate them would bring unilateral union action. At 3 p.m. union members appeared in person carrying an assortment of grievances in their teeth, demanding satisfaction from Mooncroft in his capacity as Assistant Personnel Manager. The bulk of the protests came from the firm's Tonbridge factory, where what were described at 'fascist louts' had refused to work alongside chimpanzees on the assembly-lines. A fracas had broken out after a woman supervisor complained that an orangutang had made a pass at her in the canteen, and a number of unpleasant remarks had been delivered concerning 'dirty foreign monkeys coming over here stealing our jobs and sleeping with our women'. A gorilla, acting on behalf of the Committee For Animal Equality, had thereupon thrown four welders off the roof. There were several other complaints handed to Mooncroft concerning discrimination, the inadequacy of toilet facilities for stoats, nasty practical jokes, and compensation for a donkey who had been called a communist bastard by a human colleague and had had a nervous breakdown on the shop-floor.

By the time the delegation of animals had left, Mooncroft's nerves had become frayed and tattered; he had asked for a cup of tea, but had made the mistake of sugaring it himself, and in the subsequent demarcation dispute Osric the tea-dog tore off his left trouser-leg, and a hog whose job it was to open windows handed in its notice.

Nor had the journey home been any more pleasant: for six months now, Mooncroft had been obliged to share his carriage with a group of goats who travelled daily between Cannon Street and Ilford. He had been unable to ascertain their exact status in the City, since they never did anything except stare out of the windows and eat airmail editions of *The New York Times.*

160

Gloomily he pressed his doorbell, tensed for the idiot face of Esmeralda, the Mooncrofts' sloth, who had come from Ecuador as an *au pair* and insisted on remaining with the family when her contract expired. When it had been pointed out to her that her inestimable services were no longer required, she had thrown a sofa through the living-room window and gone up to her room to watch television. She had been with them ever since and, apart from her habit of cooking such items as lightbulbs and rugs, a rude working arrangement had been arrived at. Mooncroft hated the sight of her.

He walked slowly into his home, resignedly handing his briefcase to Esmeralda (who loped off to boil it), and put his hat and umbrella carefully in the safe. His wife was waiting for him in their living-room. There was a sheep standing on the sideboard, but Mooncroft ignored it; it was immediately apparent that his wife Verbena was suffering from something far more ominous than mere quadrupeds on the furniture. She looked at him for several moments from red-rimmed eyes, not speaking. In the silence, the sheep's digestive tract murmured quietly.

'Is something wrong, Verbena?' said Mooncroft.

She blew her nose dismally.

'It's the Ryemoulds,' she said. 'They've moved out.'

The Ryemoulds had been the Mooncrofts' next-door neighbours. More, they were their closest friends.

'Just like that?' said Mooncroft.

She nodded.

'They came in this morning, just before they went. Dennis was given the sack yesterday. He's been replaced by a pig. They've had to go up north.'

Mooncroft reeled.

'But Dennis was a Grade III computer operative!' he cried. 'A salaried man! An expert!'

'I know,' sniffed Verbena Mooncroft. 'But when you boiled it all down, he was really only a button-pusher. And his firm found you could train a pig to do everything that Dennis did, for half the wages.' She wiped her eyes. 'The pig is the most intelligent of animals, Henry.'

Mooncroft paced the room, hands clasped to his ears.

'It's diabolical! It's lunatic! Where will it end? You

know they've taken on forty pekinese in our despatch office? It's disgusting, bringing cheap Chinese labour over here, putting Englishmen on the dole, disrupting the British way of life. What is to become of us, Verbena? Next thing you know, they'll be training ferrets to be Assistant Personnel Managers.' He dropped brokenly into a chair. 'Where are the children?'

'They've taken the oyster for a walk.'

'Oyster?'

'Shellfish are the only pets you're allowed to have under the Race Relations Act,' said his wife. 'I shouldn't worry, dear. They're very good with children. Very loyal.'

'I hope it's house-trained,' muttered Mooncroft. 'I've got enough to think about without following an oyster about all day, cleaning up after it. What's that noise?'

The Mooncrofts went to the window. Outside the house next door, a removal van had pulled up.

'That's quick,' said Verbena.

'I hope they're nice people,' said Mooncroft. 'Gin-rummy players. With their own lawn-mower.'

The van's tail-flap clattered open, and two gorillas got down, carrying a settee between them.

'Nice furniture, anyway,' said Verbena Mooncroft. 'Tasteful.'

They watched while bedroom suites and carpets and tables and chairs and packing-crates were unloaded and carried inside by the apes.

'When the new people turn up,' said Mooncroft, 'we'll ask them in for a sherry. It's only neighbourly.'

'They'll be along in a minute,' said Verbena. 'It's quite exciting, really. Look, the van's pulling away.'

'That's odd,' said Mooncroft. 'The gorillas are still there. On the lawn.'

'Probably waiting for the owners. Probably expect a tip.'

'Yes. Hallo, they've got a key. They're going inside.'

Nothing happened for another hour. It was not until Verbena Mooncroft went into the back room to lay the table that she became aware of a faint fluttering about the heart. From the dining-room window, she could see into the next-door garden. The two gorillas were sitting on the lawn, eating bananas.

'Henry!'

Together, they stared for some time, silently. At last, Mooncroft spoke.

'It can't be,' he whispered. 'It isn't possible. Not in this neighbourhood. Not in Ilford. Not next door.'

All evening, while the sun slowly vanished, the Mooncrofts stood there, watching. The children sat in their bedroom, playing with their oyster, oblivious to the darkening threat across the fence. The moon came up, lividly, yellowing the Mooncrofts' sickened eyes. And in Laburnum Crescent, Ilford, there was no sound at all, save for the low, ominous chuckling of anthropoid apes.

Your Teeth in Their Hands

According to a report commissioned by the General Denta Practitioners' Association, the average dentist is 'oppressed by health, ageing, status ambiguity, social paranoia and social isolation, and has become neurotic over his inability to achieve the same social recognition as the medical practitioner'. What dentistry requires, clearly, is a new Image, a Folk Myth, a Kildare or Ben Casey – in short, a Great Romantic Hero.

The Story So Far: When tall, azure-eyed, blond-haired undergrad Lord Dunromin flees Oxford two days after stroking his boat to victory, London's social world is flung into baffled misery. His unutterably beautiful fiancée model girl Princess Doreen of Labia, receives a note from the West London Air Terminal saying that Dunromin has decided to shoulder the blame for his guardsman brother's indiscretions in St. James's Park, and leave England forever. Relinquishing his title, he joins the French Foreign Legion as plain Garth Genesis, and is immediately posted to the immeasurably disgusting Fort Zinderneuf, deep in the Sahara. The camp dentist has contracted *le cafard* and pliered himself to death, and the morale of the men is exceeding low: racked by caries, halitosis, gingivitis and Bedouin tongue-acne, they are ill-equipped to defend themselves against the hordes of crazed Touaregs who, fitted out with Oxfam dentures and Czech machine-guns, are preparing for their final assault on the garrison. But they have reckoned without Garth Genesis, whose enormous (yet amazingly witty) brain has applied itself to the task of learning the dentist's art: within days, aided only by a tawny, half-naked beauty from Lille (who called at the fort

164

to sell vacuum-cleaners), Garth completely re-establishes dental hygiene among the men, working through the night by the dim light of a burning prisoner to fill holes, extract deficient molars, build sturdy bridgework until the regiment's teeth are the pride of the Legion. After the Touaregs are overwhelmingly defeated, Garth Genesis is awarded the Croix de Guerre, the Legion d'Honneur, and the B.D.S. and bar. By this time, his brother has confessed his crimes and opened fourteen male boutiques on the proceeds, whereupon Garth Genesis, after saving an upper Number Four of a visiting dignitary close to de Gaulle, is given an honourable discharge. He returns to England and a knighthood for services to Anglo-French relations, and sets up a surgery in Wimpole Street. Soon afterwards, however, a third cousin of the Queen for whom he has been designing a set of evening teeth and matching earrings, falls hopelessly in love with him and leaves her husband. *NOW READ ON:*

The Hon. Fenella Strume-Clavering's lovelorn eyes gazed down, intoxicated, as Garth Genesis's lithe fingers probed and caressed the dark, secret places of her mouth. They were the fingers of a dentist: strong, lean, tanned. Virile. Her heart pounded.

'Spit,' he said.

She turned her exquisite head, bent over the bowl, unable to spit; a single tear rolled down her nose and splashed the immaculate porcelain.

'You realise, madame,' said Genesis levelly, 'that there is absolutely nothing wrong with your teeth?'

She looked away from his unfathomable blue eyes.

'Yes,' she whispered. 'I know. But I had to come. I had –'

A bell tinkled, and Genesis sprang across to the instrument in one bound with the easy power of a panther trained to answer telephones. He listened, his fine brow furrowing.

'I'll be right over. Do nothing till I arrive.'

He replaced the receiver, and turned once more to his ravishing patient.

'That was the Chief Commissioner,' he said. 'There's a

chap at the top of the Millbank Tower threatening to throw himself off. I have to go.'

Their eyes met for an enigmatic instant, and she flashed him a brave smile which he had done so much to create. Not for nothing was he known throughout the civilised world as the Benvenuto Cellini of the platinum inlay. He turned on a handshod heel and, in a whiff of lingering halothane, was gone.

* * *

A gale was shrieking round the roof, as Garth Genesis leapt from the service elevator: only for a second did he allow himself to glance down at the minuscule details of London, four hundred teetering feet below. Then, with a cry of 'Let me through, I'm a dentist!' he plunged into the mass of doctors, archbishops, psychiatrists, journalists and back-bench politicians, all of whom instantly fell back reverently to let him pass. Beyond, at the very edge of the overhang, a man instantly recognisable as a TV personality loved by millions hovered between life and pavement. At the sight of Genesis, the matinée idol face broke into a wretched smile: the crowd gasped. Within the famous mouth, the rotted teeth hung like tiny salamis in some toy-town delicatessen. 'My career is at an end!' moaned the star; but a strong hand flew out to save and comfort. 'Nonsense!' cried the great dentist. 'Merely a case of arc-light rot. Put yourself in my hands: together we shall save you for posterity!' Weeping, the star stepped slowly back into the land of the living, and, as swiftly as he had come, Garth Genesis left once more. Behind him, the gale plucked the cheers from the mouths of tycoons and clerics and scattered them across a grateful land.

* * *

'Gargle, please!'

The Hon. Fenella Strume-Clavering dribbled miserably into the bowl, while her delectable tongue nudged numbly at the gap left by a vanished tooth. It had been a perfectly good canine, and only a fit of wild hysterics on her part had finally persuaded Genesis to extract it for what he had managed to convince himself were psychological reasons. For her, it had not seemed too high a price to pay for one more fleeting visit. She looked up at him with moist eyes.

'I hag leg my hugban!' she cried.

'Please try not to talk,' he said gently.

'You doe uggertag!' shrieked the Hon. Fenella. 'I hag leg my hugban!'

The great dentist frowned.

'You have left your husband?'

'Yeg!'

He smiled, and his splendid eyebrows rippled deliciously.

'It's merely the effect of the anaesthetic, dear lady,' he said. 'You'll feel perfectly all right in an hour or so.'

Whereupon he bowed, left her in the care of his lovely nurse, and went to keep an appointment with the Prime Minister.

* * *

'Frankly and freely,' said the Prime Minister, 'and I do mean that sincerely, I find myself, as we all do, sometimes – I'm sure you yourself do – faced with something of a problem. It's a problem in which we all have a share, it's a problem I know we can lick if we just set aside our little personal differences for a short while, and pull together in this great – and I do mean great, I mean it most sincerely – this great country of ours. Frankly, fearlessly, honestly –'

'What exactly is the problem, Prime Minister?' said Garth Genesis, from his comfortable fauteuil opposite the throne.

'It's my smile,' said the P.M.

'Your smile?'

'It's been a good smile, I won't deny that,' said the P.M. 'It's been frank, and fearless, and honest, and sincere for a good three years now, and I don't have to tell you what a strain that puts on the cheeks.'

'The burdens of office, Prime Minister.'

'Quite. But now, as we move together into the darkening storm, and the shadow of unemployment falls across this great country and my salary, I feel I need something

a little special. Something noble. Saintly, almost.'

Garth Genesis stood up and handed the P.M. his hand-tooled pattern book, indicating a couple of possible designs. The Prime Minister's tiny eyes lit up.

'Those!' he cried.

'Impeccable, Prime Minister!' said Garth Genesis. 'Joan of Arc upper plate, with a Nelson Eddy lower. And just a suggestion of Attila the Hun, perhaps, at the edges? For integrity?'

'Perfect!' cried the P.M., clapping his hands. 'Perfect! What can I offer you in return? Ask and it shall be given.'

* * *

The Hon. Fenella Strume-Clavering spat wretchedly, watched her blood swirl away into the sewage system with lead upon her heart. It was her fourteenth extraction.

'Now you're Goreign Gecretary,' she whimpered, 'I guppoge you'll gig up gentistry?'

'*Au contraire*,' said Genesis, wiping his wonderful hands on a scented towel, 'I shall always be a dentist first, and a Foreign Secretary second.' His fine eyes veiled nobly. 'Once dentistry gets into a man's blood, once he feels the pulse of the drill in his fingers, the smell of floss in his nostrils, he has given up more than his life, madame. He has given up his soul!'

The Hon. Fenella groped beneath her bloodstained gown and flung out a hand to touch his.

'Gake me wig you!' she cried. 'I lug you, Gark!'

He stepped back, hand to his brow.

'I cannot, madame! I fear that destiny has shaped me for other ends. As a statesman, nay, as a dentist, I may not allow the slightest taint to impeach my honour and the honour of my calling! Return to your husband! Return to your little ones!' He paused a moment, and glanced down at his distracted slave. 'Besides, madame, have I not this very instant removed your last remaining natural tooth? How could you thus take your place beside me, the first dental Foreign Secretary the world has ever seen, and you with nought but a mouthful of gums?'

With an unearthly, fearful shriek, the Hon. Fenella

Strume-Clavering cast off her gown and staggered from the chair that had borne her through so many long years of unrequited passion. The surgery doors swung shut, and her gummy moans faded on the Marylebone air.

But the Rt. Hon. Garth Genesis, B.D.S., heeded them not. Bathed in the roseate glow of an English evening, his handsome form stood silhouetted in the surgery window, gazing out upon the teeth and embassies that awaited him, somewhere beyond the setting sun.

Some talk of Alexander, and some of Hercules: but me, I've been strolling the boulevards this past week whistling *Puppet On A String* till my teeth are falling about in my head like skittles. And dared any dago cross my path without giving due attention to his forelock, I'd have had my malacca cane across his bonce before you could say Rudyard Palmerston.

Moan not for long-lost Mandelays! Stub out the lingering embers of nostalgia for Cairo and Rangoon! What boots it to grieve for the thin red lines of yesteryear with breath that would be better spent in cheering Sandie Shaw? Smile through your tears, lads, the European Song Contest is ours at last! A new Britain is without, striding across the threshold to a new Elizabethan Age fit to make the last lot look like a scratch matinée at the Hackney Empire.

Not, of course, that it wasn't touch, and even go. My wife and I, together with other loyal supporters of the empire on which the sun never rises, were down at London Airport to see Sandie off. Many of the lads were in old tattered uniforms of brave regiments long defunct, and the curious appropriateness of the gear brought a crystal drop to many a life-hardened eye; strong men from Guildford sobbed, and redfaced Cornish farmers beat their breasts as the great jets fired and Rock Bottom's Psychedelic Flock struck up *I Was Lord Kitchener's Valet* on their jerry-cans.

It was a tremulous moment, as the great silver bird trundled forward. Would this be another Munich? Could He that made the lamb look the wrong way at the vital moment? Would, in short, the wops, frogs, coolies and other E.E.C. reptilia fail to be smitten with Sandie? Would they root instead for some inferior local glottis, damning Britain yet again to the dank humiliation of other years, hurling Sandie back across the Channel, like so many before her, forcing her into the oblivion of an Esher bungalow and spasmodic commercials for cheap deodorant?

Ugly rumours whistled around Heathrow as the plane vanished, winking, into the fateful murk: the judges were all Gaullists, ex-Nazis, Rhodesians in false moustaches and sombreros; the crowd, minds teeming with memories of Trafalgar and Mersah Matruh, of cut-price tourists on the Costa Brava, of the degradation of the World Cup, of the *Sunday Times* exposé of Beaujolais, would shout Sandie down, throw ravioli, unplug her microphone; Greek Cypriots would release trained Eoka mice across the stage, expatriate Egyptians would chuck small, sharp pieces of Port Said at the lights, Baldur von Schirach would hold a rally in the biergarten opposite.

But they didn't. Just before midnight, while all the world wondered, the news came through. Blinded by mad, forgivable tears and unable to see anything of the telly but a shifting puddle of pale grey ectoplasm, we heard the announcer choke out the incredible news. Britain, which only nineteen hundred years before had been locked in a historical impasse of woad and illiteracy, had come from behind to snatch the greatest prize the civilised world can offer. After a short, yet pithy prayer, I helped my wife to her feet and together we opened the windows: all across London, bathed in a soft sodium blush beneath our feet, we could hear the sound of cheering. It was all going to be all right. Over towards Finchley, a single rocket soared into the sky and burst in violet rain. Many of us found God, that night.

No need to remind you of the ecstasy with which our great British press fell upon the magnificent news! From Printing House Square to the meanest village broadsheet, the triumph of British songwriting and songsinging was writ large, thrusting the ephemeral trivia of Vietnam and Aden into the corners they deserved. The triumphal return of Sandie (self-confessedly, but forgivably sloshed) laden with exotic flora in the diminutive yet still-popular arms of Adam Faith (the Biblical overtones did not pass unnoticed by us devotees of the swinging Book), was a sight for sore lenses, and no art editor worth his fixing salt passed up the opportunity to share in England's glory.

To judge from the shimmering verbiage of the teenage journalists who flocked to their Olivettis on the morrow morn, the effect on Britain's international prestige would be electrifying, not to say (though everyone did) psychedelic. Already, in far veldt and atoll, the darkies were stripping off their new bowlers and constitutions and practising their vocal versions of the Colonial Cringe, squinting spasmodically at the sky in anticipation of descending bwanas in op-art pith helmets and electronic bugles.

'Look here, upon this picture, and on this!' cried my wife, rattling a fistful of national dailies. 'They say that Sandie's magnificent triumph could mean a twenty per cent increase in exports of le mini-jupe alone! Not to mention the opening-up of vast new markets for such items as silver-kid boots, mod cosmetics, gold lamé stockings and joke jewellery!'

'Wonderful!' I cried, 'Wonderful!' My eyes filled again with tears at the thought of emaciated tots running about in the Kalahari, naked save for their silver-kid boots, laughing themselves sick over their joke earrings, eagerly putting their shaky crosses to plebiscites demanding the return of British Colonial Authority before the night was out.

'English hair-styling, too, should benefit,' she read, stifling a joyous sob.

'Ha! Let FLOSY bite on that for a minute!' I shouted. 'Any more foul language in the Crater District, and we'll send a hairdresser up the Gulf!'

Could there be any greater vindication of Young Britain than this? A new cultural and colonial revolution to hold the world in awe, a return of Britannia's dusky children to their preordained fold, the flag lowered by loyal souls in far tropical evenings to the muted strains of *Penny Lane* played on an old kazoo, the clink of British necklaces in the outposts of empire, Vidal

Sassoon horse-hair wigs hanging beside the shrunken heads in the Borneo swamps, dervishes in their mini-burnooses freaking out amid the shimmering sands, delirious with cool mirages of Radio Caroline bobbing off the coast of Mother England. Ah, Sandie, heiress of Drake and Clive and Gordon, up what new Heights of Abraham may you not lead us now? *Dulce et decorum est pro patria canere,* baby, and don't you forget it: leave us not slacken at the helm, with all the world in fee!

I hope only that her example will be followed, and followed quickly. That *Come Dancing* will extend its competitive area to include all Europe – ach! to out-tango the Spaniard, to out-waltz the smug Viennese! That English red-nosed comics will sow the seeds of insecurity in every music-hall in the world; that British spoons-players and one-string fiddlers will captivate the queues of Portugal and Greece; that Percy Edwards and Ronnie Ronalde will charm the vulture and the emu with their incomparable whistling; that Smith and Vorster will fall in their peoples' clamouring for nationwide tours by the Black And White Minstrels.

We shall not flag or fail. We shall smite the infidel hip and thigh with Engelbert Humperdinck and *Carry On Nurse,* with Lionel Blair and *Juke Box Jury*, with More-cambe, Wise, and Twiggy. This is not the end. It is not even the beginning of the end. But it is, perhaps, the end of the beginning.

Dem Words, Dem Words,
Gonna Walk Aroun'

'Corgi Books, one of the biggest paperback publishers in Britain, is being taken over by an American film, theatre and TV company as part of a £20,000,000 deal. A director said yesterday that he expected the deal to lead to film and book tie-ups. "This is a marvellous thing for us," he said, "we will be able to send our books to America for film ideas".'   **The Times**

It had been a great week at Mongrel Books: even those members of the board whose memories stretched back over months of publishing were agreed on that. On Monday, after a thrilling financial tussle between several hysterical bidders (including a national chain of fishmongers who planned to flood the market with novels about roe, and a millionaire vegetarian dermatologist who had cornered the market in unpublished autobiographies of millionaire vegetarian dermatologists), the company was at last knocked down to Rank Fox Pictures (Hollywood) Inc., the largest film/stage/television consortium in the world.

On Tuesday, the new owners had initiated a literacy test for the executive staff, most of whom had passed with flying colours and thereupon been assigned to exciting duties in the packing department. On Wednesday, their places were immediately filled with a swinging battalion of teenage financial wizards, shirt manufacturers, casting directors, pop painters, discotheque magnets, public re-

174

lations geniuses, and a select group of the more famous hair stylists. On Thursday, David Hockney and the Duke of Bedford came in and decorated the offices in trendy khaki straw and broken plates, and in the evening everyone appeared on *The Frost Programme* in time to make the morning editions, which, by sheer chance, also carried full-page advertisements showing nude crowned heads of Europe reading Mongrel Books on the steps of the Vatican. On Saturday, everyone in N.W.1. signed a further full-page advertisement in *The Times* defending the right of Mongrel Books to put full-page advertisements in *The Times*. On the sixth day they rested, and on Monday they opened for business.

Hardly had managing-director Savonarola Loines (né J. F. Tibbs) slid into official position behind the onyx acreage of his desk, when the doors of his suite flew open to admit two of the most wonderful people in the world. Dismissing his manicurist, and adjusting his dress, Loines sprang forward to greet them.

'Why!' he cried, 'surely it's fabulous twelve-year-old model girl Weeny?'

'That's right,' said her agent.

'And her miraculous agent Fats Ariosto!' cried Loines, embracing him with an authenticity that belied his tender years. 'What can we at Rank Fox Mongrel Inc. do for you beautiful people?'

'Weeny done a book,' said her agent.

'A book! All on her own?'

'Show him the script,' said the agent.

The minuscule celebrity opened her gold-lamé Bonny Parker machine-gun case and produced a sheet of paper covered in scrawled lipstick. Very slowly, lurching at every disyllable, she began, in fashionable Cockney, to read:

> 'She dwelt among the untrodden ways
>   Beside the springs of Dove,
> A maid whom there were none to praise
>   And very few to love:
>
> A violet by a mossy stone
>   Half Hidden from the eye.

Fair as a star, when only one
    Is shining in the sky.

She lived unknown, and few could know
    When Lucy ceased to be;
    But she is in her grave, and, oh,
    The difference to me!'

'Fantastic!' shouted Loines. 'She wrote that herself?'

'The lot,' said Fats Ariosto. 'Copied it all down in her own hand, just like that. Got it out of this old book we found up Camden Passage. Course, I 'ad to 'elp her with joining the letters up, din't I? She don't do real writing till next term, but she prints a fair treat.'

'Amazing!' said Loines. 'Mind you, it's a bit short for a novel. But it's all there, it's all packed in, it's real life, know what I mean? We'll just have to fill it out a bit, large print, lots of lovely psychedelic pix, and nice big photos of Weeny.'

'And me.'

'And you, naturally. I see a sort of luminous laminated plastic cover, with you and Weeny frugging in Poets' Corner, something like that. Go like a bomb. We'll start off with a print order for a million. What about the disc?'

'Disc?'

'To be released simultaneous with publication. These days, kids like a book with a nice tune. Something they can dance to.'

'I was thinking more about the film,' said Fats Ariosto. The sun peeped out suddenly from behind a cloud, and, with a lightning flick, the agent changed wigs. 'That and the telly series.'

Loines smiled reassuringly.

'Leave all that with me,' he said. 'Why not just get your accountant to drop in on our contract department, and let us take it from there? We'll keep in touch.'

The wonderful couple slouched out, passing as they did so a small, round man in a chintz suit and smoked bifocals, who hove to alongside Loines's desk. The managing-director passed him the Weeny masterpiece. Minutes passed filled with low, sibilant breathing.

'Well?' said Loines at last. 'Any angles?'

'It's beautiful,' said the round man. 'I see Lucy dolls, and Lucy fun hairpieces, and a whole range of Lucyline lipsticks, and Lucy see-through mini-culottes, and Lucy shoe-trees, and maybe we should open a couple of Lucy bistros here and there, and then there's bathroom fittings and . . .'

'It sounds great, Mitzo,' said Loines, who was on his feet again, gathering papers into his douche-bag. 'I'll leave it with you, baby. If you need me, I'll be in Hollywood.'

A mere twelve hours later, Loines found himself sweating in a private Turkish bath in Bel Air, beside the shining feet of the head of Rank Fox himself. Above him, the pearly skin of the great impresario faded into the boiling mist, and his voice rolled down from the high invisible mouth for all the world like God, or even Charlton Heston.

'It's a beautiful story, Savonarola,' said the great man. 'Beautiful. Cinemascope was made for this. We'll call it *Whatever Happened To Mossy Stone?* That's the kind of title they go for these days. You know, like long.'

Loines blinked the sweat from his eyes.

'Mossy Stone?'

'You got it. He's this sympathetic Jewish fighter-pilot she meets in hospital in Vietnam where she's gone to give this heart transplant to a needy orphan. He – Mossy – used to be this great saxophonist, see, before he was drafted, only the Cong broke his fingers on account he wouldn't tell them where the gold was hidden. I see Kirk Douglas. Mastroianni.'

'It sounds great,' said Loines, furiously adapting the idea for the musical stage in his head. 'But how does she get to Vietnam in the first place?'

'It's like this,' said the voice above. 'The way I see it, the important figure is the "me" in the last line, right? I mean the narrator, this cat who goes to pieces when Lucy gets the pine-box treatment in the line before. Naturally, this is Sidney Poitier, who was always in the background, I mean always carrying this big torch for Lucy, only he couldn't marry her on account she's black.'

'Sidney couldn't marry her because she's *black*?'

'Right. Since when did Sidney get tangled up with a black

girl? It so happens he only digs the pale people, see, but he realises he loves Lucy only after she taps out. We open on this foxhole outside Da Nang, and Sidney's telling the story to a representative group of G.I.'s – an Eyetie, a big Swede, two Irishmen, Mossy Stone's brother the lawyer, and a South Korean kid Gene Kelly brought up after his parents got knocked off in the Korean war. We have this flashback of them dancing together, before Gene tells the kid he has an incurable wasting disease and is going to see the kid's Mummy and Daddy in the big paddy-field in the sky.'

'I like it,' cried Loines, calculating the income from serial rights rapidly, 'I like it.'

'So anyway, Sidney tells them how he met this broad in the Springs of Dove, which is this underwater nightclub in Acapulco where she's working as a hoofer to raise the money for lawyers to get her old man the nuclear physicist off this charge of working for the Reds he's been framed for. Like the books says, she's a maid whom there were none to praise, on account she's this lousy dancer, and don't even sell cigarettes good. She has a spot singing "Few To Love" which is all about how all the clients are always making out with her, only no one loves her for herself, see? Maybe they think she's working for the Reds, too, something like that. We'll leave the interpretation to Liz.'

'Taylor?'

'Who else? Then one day, this very old gunfighter rides into town – '

'Gunfighter? In 1969?'

'I mean, like *real* old – we see this flashback where he's learning to shoot from Wyatt Earp. They stick these cans on a fence. Only now he's ninety-seven, and he's kind of sick of killing, and everything. I see Randolph Scott in the part, we'll make him up to look younger, know what I mean?'

'It sounds great up to now, B. J.,' said Loines. 'What next?'

'Well, that's as far as I got, just off the top of my head,' said the great man. 'Somewhere we got to get in these talking animals. I hear *Dolittle*'s already grossed seven million.

The important thing is, we never clear up the question of how Lucy gets into the grave, and why it makes this big difference to Sidney. We keep them guessing, right?'

'For the T.V. series?'

'Right! Also the cartoon-strip, which is about Lucy's early life on a Japanese baby-farm where this Samurai stud keeps on . . .'

The telephone rang, and Loines leapt to answer. He listened long, scribbling furiously on a shorthand pad. When he hung up, his face gleamed with more than mere perspiration.

'That was Weeny's agent,' he cried. 'She just wrote a sequel. Get this, B.J.: "I wandered lonely as a cloud that floats on high o'er vales and hills, when all at once . . . " '

The rolls of fat above Savonarola Loines shook with excitement.

'Fantastic!' cried the great man. 'It's about this astronaut, right?'

'It is? I mean, right, B.J., right!'

'It's about this coloured Catholic kid from a broken home, all he dreams of is being the first man on the moon, only – does it have a title yet?'

'Well, they didn't actually say, but . . .'

A great hand materialised suddenly out of the swirling steam, and slapped joyfully against a giant thigh.

'What else?' cried the great man. 'We'll call it *Whatever Happened To The Son Of Mossy Stone*?'

Cheap At Any Price

I was hunched beneath the bonnet of my car, trying to pull off something flash with the plugs and a sliver of sandpaper, when a fat black shadow fell across the engine. I screwed my head round, to find beside me the ill-assorted body of my next-door neighbour, a short Williams Pear of a man whom every tailor north of the Thames has come to think of as the little rain which into each sartorial life must fall. Normally, the fact is well-enough disguised beneath expensive tweed and hopsack, but on this occasion, the layers of heaving blubber laboured under a bright white T-shirt, sloppy at the shoulders, tight as a wineskin at the navel. Nor was this all. In loose, distorted lettering between the tiny offensive peaks of his ambiguous breasts, ran the legend: *REGENT*, across the red-and-blue symbol of the Regent Oil Company. His eyes caught mine, and misinterpreted the horror there.

'Great, isn't it?' he said. 'Three-and-six, that's all. When you fill up with Regent, that is. At your friendly neighbourhood Regent station. Worth all of seven bob.'

'It's very nice,' I said.

'Soon as there's a bit of space in the tank,' he said, 'the wife's going to have one, too. Matching, get it?'

The picture of the pair of them, like small soft bookends, shrieked in my mind briefly, but I held my smile.

'That shouldn't take you long,' I said. 'Quick bomb down the North Circular and back'll use up a couple of gallons.'

'Ah, well,' he said. 'It's a question of priorities. I mean, Regent's got to take its turn, hasn't it?'

180

He slid away on this enigma, opened his garage, and backed his car onto the forecourt. I hadn't seen it for some time, and was consequently unprepared for the shock: every window was filled with simulated bullet-holes, the back bumper was a solid mass of luminous slogans, and three tiger-tails hung from the boot. The thing appeared to be the property of some advertising man who had been caught trapping animals in Kruger National Park and had only escaped capture by running a gauntlet of game-wardens' sten-guns.

'That's quite a collection,' I said, when he got out to shut his garage. He beamed, and fingered a tyre-company pennant hanging from his aerial.

'Yes. 'Course, it's got its drawbacks. From behind, you can't see the dangle-dollies for the bullet-holes, and with the slogan on the windscreen, I can only overtake things by leaning forward and looking through the steering-wheel.'

'Why have a slogan on the windscreen, then?' I said.

'Ah, well, there's no more room on the bumpers, is there?' He smiled at the neatness of this unanswerable logic, and smoothed the wrinkles from an anti-freeze label that the summer months had unthinkingly ravaged. 'You don't pay a penny for any of these, you know. You just ask. I've known places where they don't even take the cost of your stickers out of your double green stamps special offer for over four gallons. Mind you,' he went on, 'it's not all as easy as it looks.'

He cradled my elbow in plump fingers and drew me to the mouth of his garage. Inside, neatly stacked, were some ten jerrycans of petrol, and a dozen or so cans of lubricating-oil.

'I'm at a disadvantage over your big-car owner,' said my neighbour. 'I mean, I got one of these damn economy cars, forty to the gallon, thousand miles to the pint of oil – I got enough stuff there to get me to Istanbul. Whereas there's this friend of mine, got a 1951 Princess, does ten to the gallon, petrol or oil, don't matter which. He's had four free beach-balls, a rubber dinghy, and all his kids have got three T-shirts apiece. Not to mention the green stamps – he's well on his way to an electro-plated barbecue-pit, provided the bastards from the M.O.T. don't take his car off the road before October.'

'You mean,' I said, 'that you're actually storing petrol in cans?'

'Well, that's one way of looking at it,' he said. 'Thing is, I've only got a seven-gallon tank, see? Now, when it comes to your Shell Great Miracle Offer, I'm in the cart, aren't I? I mean, most garages expect you to put in at least a gallon of the stuff before they'll cough up the Special Sealed Envelope containing half a ten-bob voucher, or half a hundred quid, or whatever it is. I'm only getting about four envelopes a week, and they're all bloody left-handers. What's the odds on me picking up both halves of a hundred? Whereas some bloke with a Rolls must be cleaning up, right?' He looked at his tiny car bitterly. 'It's one law for the rich and one for the poor. Still, it'll be all right when I've got the four-and-a-half litre vintage Bentley.'

'I had no idea you were interested in buying old cars,' I said.

'*Buying?* I'm not slinging *my* money away, mate. Not on a load of old brass headlamps and chromium plumbing. No it's Mobilgas, got this competition, see? What you do is, you fill up with Mobilgas, and you get a free vintage-car cigarette-card. When you've got a complete set, you send up for a free album, stick 'em all in, then you send up the album for a free go trying to win a free vintage car. Piece of cake.' He smiled cannily, and tapped the side of his gleaming nose. 'Then, soon as I've got this free car well, it's doing about four miles to the gallon, right? So off I go to the *Shell* stations, picking up left and right-hand halves willy-nilly.'

'It's a great scheme,' I said.

He smiled modestly.

'It's the wife's actually. She fancies the idea of living in a twenty-thousand-pound dream house.'

'I'm sorry?'

'Esso,' he said. He stared at me curiously. 'Don't you *read*, or something? Esso have got this competition to win a twenty-thousand-quid house. Of your choice. Anywhere in England. I don't know how they manage to make ends meet, I swear I don't, giving all this clobber away. As soon as I've cashed in all the vouchers I've got from Shell for buying petrol for this Mobilgas Bentley I'm getting, I'll have the money to buy *more* petrol for both cars, see? And every time I fill up with Esso, I'll cop one of the free entry forms for their dream house contest.' His small eyes glazed for a moment. 'We're wondering where's the best place to build, as a matter of fact. The wife's always going on about Frinton, but it's a bit quiet for me. I mean, I like to be near garages, and everything. You can never tell what you might miss, stuck down at Frinton. They might start giving away helicopters or yachts, or something. I fancy a little place just off the M4, actually. Somewhere like Maidenhead, near a service area. Marvellous things, those Motorway service areas – got all brands, anything you like, all the entry forms and stickers and stuff, all in little boxes on the walls, you can take your pick. Modern.'

He walked away, shaking his head among his dreams, and slammed his garage door. He was on the point of getting into his Mini, when a high shriek split the morning just behind us, and I turned to see his spherical wife rolling across the asphalt, waving and gibbering.

'What is it?' he shouted.

She teetered up and leaned breathlessly against his car, fanning her face with a Surf coupon.

'Shopping,' she gasped. She fell into a desperate coughing fit, while we waited, rattled to a halt, and smiled at me apologetically. 'Sorry,' she said, 'I've just taken up smoking for the coupons, and sixty a day's all I can manage without falling down, but it still gets me here.' She tapped her undulating bosom feebly. 'It's those first ten before breakfast that's the worst, isn't it?'

'What about the shopping, then?' said her husband impatiently.

She took the handkerchief from her lips.

'I meant to tell you,' she croaked, 'not to get the Free Bermuda Holiday jar of Nescafe.'

'I thought you fancied Bermuda.'

'I do, it's just that if you get a Giant Economy Tide instead, there's a free green plastic bowl goes with it.'

Without another word, her husband leapt into his car,

183

spun backwards, and roared off towards town. I looked at her.

'But do you *need* a green plastic bowl?' I asked.

'Oh, yes,' she said. 'It'll come in ever so handy for keeping the Pink Stamps in.'

Something About a Soldier

'*A team of investigators has shown that of all the men who wear regimental ties, six in ten are probably imposters.*'
Daily Mirror

Thomas Breen laid his green leatherette sample-case care-fully in the boot of the company Cortina; shut the lid; locked it. You couldn't be too careful, not with the electric toothbrushes. Valuable items like that, and the country the way it was, no morals any more and much of it black. He crossed the carpark, gravel grinding under his brogues, a march step, firm and dependable, can't beat good real leather on your soles, none of your pansy composite, and stepped, smartly, through the saloon lounge door, mascu-line stride across the figured pile, shoulders fat (but square) belly held in, small smile beneath the smaller moustache, and the wide green goldstripe tie trumpeting on his chest.

'Good morning, sir.'

'It is, indeed! Bright. But not sunny. It'll be taking spin.'

'Sir?'

'The wicket. Bit green after the rain. Taking spin. Definitely. Skittle 'em out by tea. Or soon after.'

'What can I get you, sir?'

'Pink gin. Large.'

Thomas Breen sniffed, twitched his bristles, cleared his throat.

'Ice?'

Short nod, chins interfolding briefly.

'Tight cap this, sir. Can't remember the last time I had to unscrew the pink. Customers don't seem to drink it these days.'

185

'Old habit,' said Breen. He chuckled. 'Medicinal. Not,' he added, leaning slightly towards the barman, humorously, 'that there's much beri-beri round here, eh?'

'Sir?'

Breen slid the bitterness down his throat, and pushed his glass back across the counter.

'Army joke. Same again. Gin for the malaria, Angostura for the beri-beri. That's what we used to say. Bit before your time.'

'I dare say, sir.'

'White man's grave, Burma,' said Breen, allowing his eyes to glaze. 'But a clever little devil, your Jap. Get him in a corner, fights like a rat.'

'Really, sir?'

'Like a ruddy rat. Have something yourself. Yes, many's the time I had to go in with cold steel and finish off some yellow johnny fighting on with half a dozen rounds still in him. Wouldn't lie down.'

'Amazing.'

'Wouldn't lie down. Once – I'm not boring you? – once, down near the Foonsang Delta, rainy season, my chaps were pinned down under a withering –'

Breen's voice frayed, and stopped. Beside him at the bar, a tall bony figure had materialised, grey-suited with a tangerine rose in his buttonhole, yellow gloves. And a green goldstriped tie. The two men looked at one another, and the pupils ran around their eyes like trapped ants.

'I say!' said Breen.

'Ha, ha!' said the newcomer.

The barman smiled, with all the bonhomie of his calling.

'Here's a turn-up,' he said. 'Same regiment! This gentleman,' he continued, drawing a beer for the newcomer, 'was just telling me about your lot in Burma.'

'Burma?' said the newcomer.

'Only there a week or so,' said Breen quickly. 'Didn't get much chance to meet anyone, ha-ha-ha! Went down with trench foot second week.'

'Trench foot?'

'Mouth. Flown back to Catterick right away.'

'Catterick, eh?'

'Only for the day. Baffled Medical Corps. Didn't see a

186

soul I knew. Driven straight to an isolation unit.'

The new man drank half his beer and put down the glass.

'Never saw Burma,' he said. He took out a handkerchief and mopped his forehead, despite the coolness of the day. Breen unclenched his hands, and licked a bright bead from his moustache.

'Really?' he said. 'Ah, well, they shipped me back there, soon as I'd recovered. Hardly saw anywhere else.'

'Weren't in Libya, then?' said the new man.

'Libya?'

'Or do I mean Palestine? I mean, I do. I say, I reckon the old wicket's due to take a bit of spin this morning, don't you? Not that I think the Australians have sent us much of a –'

A third man entered; took off his coat; revealed a wide green gold-striped tie.

'Palestine, did you say?' he asked, looking at them uneasily.

'Libya, actually,' said the second man quickly. 'I was shorter then, of course. Sprang up after I was thirty. Fingleton,' he added desperately, extending a wet hand.

'Breen,' said Breen.

'Wittle,' said the third man.

'Not Charlie Wittle,' said Fingleton, 'by any chance?'

'NO!' shouted Wittle. 'I mean, no. No, they sent *Charlie* Wittle to Libya, I suppose, I mean yes, they did, I remember that on the postings, yes, he went to Libya, and I went to, er, Burma.'

'There's a coincidence!' cried Fingleton. 'Breen here –'

'Just missed you!' exclaimed Breen. I remember, it was the day they were flying me home with foot and mouth, and they came in and said, there's a new chap just been sent out, chap called Wittle, pity you've missed him. That's what they said.'

'Breen went back, though,' insisted Fingleton, 'after he was well.'

'I would have been gone by then,' said Wittle, hurling a large Scotch down his gullet, somewhat erratically.

'Yes!' shouted Breen, 'I remember, I got off the plane, and they said, 'you've just missed Wittle again, he's gone. That's what they said.'

'Did they?' enquired Wittle, staring at him. 'Oh. Yes, well, I got posted back in time for Salerno.'

Breen and Fingleton breathed out. Everyone smiled.

'Parachuted in,' explained Wittle.

Everyone nodded. Fingleton bought another round.

'One of our regulars was at Salerno,' said the barman pleasantly. 'With your lot.' Six eyes fixed on him from the rims of their drinks. 'Major Moult. Often mentions – well, talk of the devil!'

'Breen,' murmured Breen.

'Fingleton.'

'Wittle.'

'Moult.'

'I was telling the gentlemen, Major,' said the barman, taking Moult's pewter tankard from its hook, 'about Salerno.'

'Yes,' said Breen happily, 'Wittle parachuted in, you know.'

Moult looked at Wittle.

'I didn't know there were any parachute landings at Salerno,' he said.

'Ah, well you wouldn't, old man,' said Wittle, laughing lightly, despite a shoeful of beer. 'Typical R.A.F. cock-up, ha-ha-ha! Wrong prevailing winds. All baled out over the jolly old target area, and landed forty miles away.'

'I suppose you managed to make your way back to re-join the regiment, though,' said Fingleton, 'didn't you, Wittle?'

'I would have been out of it by then,' said Moult. 'Got taken prisoner first day, shipped out to Deutschland, chop-chop.'

'Not a P.O.W. of the Jerries, were you?' said a new voice.

The four men turned, to find a short wiry man in a camelhair coat and a brown fedora. Between the smooth lapels of the former gleamed two gold bars, on a green ground.

'I escaped almost immediately,' said Moult, very loudly. 'Why did they get you, Mr –'

'Binns. Didn't they get any of the rest of you, then?'

The others shook their heads.

'They got me, all right,' said Binns confidently. 'In Libya.'

'Fingleton was in Libya,' said Wittle.

'Yes,' said Fingleton, 'I came after you were captured. Got sent out from Palestine to replace you. Jerry's got Binns, they said. You'll have to go out to Libya. That's what they said.'

Binns looked at him.

'You sure they said Binns?' he said.

Fingleton eased his tie-knot.

'Er yes,' he muttered. 'Go out and replace, er, Erasmus Binns.'

A shadow lifted from Binns's face.

'Different chap,' he said. 'I'm *Arthur* Binns. Not, of course,' he added hurriedly, 'that I haven't heard of Erasmus Binns.'

'Have you?' asked Fingleton.

'Of course, he wasn't in Libya at the *exact* same time as I was,' said Binns. 'I think he was in Burma, then.'

'That's it!' cried Fingleton. 'He was in Burma before he went to Libya and got captured and put in a P.O.W. camp.'

'After I'd escaped,' said Moult.

'He was probably in Burma about the time you were,' said Fingleton to Breen.

'Just missed him,' said Breen. 'I remember, it was the week I got dysentery, after I got back from Catterick and missed Wittle again. You've just missed Erasmus Binns, they said. As I got off the plane. They've sent him to Libya, they said.'

'Terrible thing, Burmese dysentery.'

'Who said that?' shrieked Breen, knocking over his fourth gin.

'I did.'

The group was joined by a large bald man in a black jacket, set off with green and goldstriped tie. Breen grabbed his sleeve.

'They cocked up my diagnosis!' he shouted. 'What I actually had was phosgene poisoning. Not like you at all. Nothing like it.'

'I wasn't in Burma,' said the bald man carefully.

'None of us were in Palestine,' offered Moult.

'I would have seen you if you had been,' said the bald man. 'I was there for the duration.'

'Fingleton said he'd been in Palestine,' said Breen. 'Didn't you?'

'No! Libya. With the other Wittle, not this one. Erasmus Wittle. If I said Palestine, I meant I'd *passed through it*. At night. On the train.'

'I recall that train,' said the bald man, licking a dry lip. 'I remember someone saying, Fingleton's on that train. Going to Libya.'

'That's it!' cried Fingleton. 'That's exactly it!'

The bar clock struck three.

'Time please, gentlemen,' said the barman.

The six, as one man, flung themselves at the door, bound for their cars and freedom. Their escape, however, was cut off by a group of four men, waiting quietly outside the saloon bar: two had lost a leg, a third had an empty sleeve pinned across his chest, and was playing *Tipperary*, one-handed, on a harmonica, to the banjo accompaniment of the men on crutches. A fourth man held a white stick in one hand, and a collection box in the other. All wore campaign stars; and wide green goldstriped ties.

Fingleton pulled Breen towards him.

'Look at that,' he muttered. 'Begging!'

'Disgusting!' said Breen. He felt for his car-keys. 'Don't know what the Regiment's coming to.'

The Professional Touch

A Tale of Open Wimbledon

Say what you like about professional tennis, it brings out the best in people. Take Gus Rappaport. Normally, you ask Gus Rappaport the time of day, he'll tell you it's two-thirty-three when it's really only two-thirty, on account of he reckons you owe him three minutes interest on a deal like that. Tighter than Gus Rappaport you won't find. But yesterday I'm standing around outside the Centre Court, fingering the draw and wondering what I fancy, when who comes up to me but Gus Rappaport, in a very chic mohair suit, you can tell it's imported, and wearing this big smile with a fringe of strawberry pips round it, and cream all over his moustache.

'Hallo, Gus,' I say, very cautious, not wishing to push off with any enquiry, such as How's tricks? on account of it could end up costing.

'Great,' he says, 'great. You want a hot tip?'

I pretend I don't hear. Believe me, it's better that way.

'Lew Hoad,' says Gus. 'Lew Hoad in the two o'clock, on Number One Court. Past the post. Money in the bank. No argument.'

'Hoad?' I say, overcome that Gus should be giving away such information, if genuine, when I personally know Hoad to be a nice long price, owing to the boys having looked him over in training and he is sweating too much, and puffing like my grandmother's samovar, she should rest in peace, and is generally looking like a definite non-seed. 'They tell me Hoad is off form.'

Gus looks very hurt.

'They? So who's they all of a sudden? Listen, this is Gus Rappaport, never knowingly undersold, and I'm telling you if you want to put ten on Hoad at two o'clock, by half-past you got yourself forty. I know the man who strings his rackets. I know the man who makes his supporters. Better information you won't find.

'In half an hour?' I say. 'This is a very good outsider he's matched with, Gus. Word is, the kid takes him in the fifth.'

'What fifth? This one doesn't go the distance, baby, believe me. Hoad is a hot property. He didn't get beaten in his last four outings. So he puffs a bit in training, so what? This is for the press, so they build up some story about how he's over the hill. What's with you, you should listen to such stories? I tell you, Hoad takes the kid in the third, no argument.'

Then he's gone, with a dame she's a head taller than he is, and real class, a genuine Lebanese stripper, works for only the best. I tell you, this year you got a different crowd of people at Wimbledon altogether. The cream.

So anyway, I think What can I lose? so I do Hoad for a pony in the two o'clock, and may I be struck dead if he doesn't lead from the off and come home at four to one! Like a three-year-old. 6–2, 6–3, 6–0. Like Gus says, no argument.

Naturally, this makes me somewhat happy, and as I don't fancy nothing in the next thing, it being a match between a couple of Swedes on which nobody has any information, I decide to put on a basin of strawberries and study the form for the ladies' doubles, when who do I see in the tent but Nat Bladder, and he is looking like a man who's just gone into partnership with his brother-in-law.

'So what's the trouble, Nat?' I say, through my spoon.

'Don't ask,' he says.

I put down my plate, and immediately the wasps form a queue in front of it.

'Nat,' I say, very serious, 'I know you a long time, and secrets from one another we never had. Me you can tell.'

'It's my boy,' he says. Heavy like lead.

This, you have to understand, is not his son he is referring to, with whom he also has troubles, naturally, but his protegé. The kid he manages. I know this at once, because for the past six months Nat eats and drinks this kid, telling everyone about how the boy is the hottest number in tennis since Jean Borotra's grandmother, and how the singles title is as good as on his mantelpiece. Personally, I always figure Nat's boy for a non-starter, on account of he's the only dark horse at Wimbledon who actually looks like a dark horse. I seen him in practice in Regent's Park, and first off I thought he had four legs. All left. Added to which he's around four feet tall, the whole assembly stopping just short of the brain: a few more inches on the top of his skull and they could have squeezed in something to think with, only they skimped. Naturally, I say nothing about this to Nat, because he has this dream of finding the Great White Hope and everything, and I reckon he'll find out for himself soon enough.

'So what's with the boy?' I ask, knowing the kid is scheduled to appear in the five o'clock, on about Court Eight Hundred, which is probably nearer Tooting than Wimbledon, on account of the organisers of the tournament don't want the show to get a bad name.

'I think he's planning to take a dive,' says Nat.

At this, I have to ram a couple of waspy berries into my face quick so as not to get hysterics. Not that the idea of throwing a match is so incredible – this Wimbledon it's happening all the time, believe me – it's just the thought of it mattering whether Nat's boy takes a dive or not, owing to the fact that even with nobody at the other end he'd have his work cut out to get into the first two. In fact, from what I hear around and about, any money riding on this match is going on whether Nat's kid manages to learn how to get his racket out of the press, and that's all.

'It couldn't be, Nat,' I say. 'You taught that kid everything he knows.'

After that, me and Nat look at one another for a bit. I grab my hat.

'Maybe we should go and have a talk with him, at that,' I say.

We run down the corridor towards the changing-rooms, with some difficulty due to the place being full of tennis fans in dark glasses and homburg hats, and these are not citizens you push around if you wish to keep that schoolgirl complexion. The kid is sitting on the masseur's table, trying to count five ten-pound notes, and beside him are two very wide men I immediately recognise as recently imported Sicilian sportslovers.

'Kid!' cries Nat, shaking his product like a rat. 'What did you do to me?'

At this, the larger of the mafiosi gathers the majority of Nat Bladder into one fist, draws him close, and smiles, very golden.

'Iffa you know woss good for you an' your fren,' he says, 'you woan go innerterferin witha this business arrangement wot I justa done.'

'You erd wotty say,' says his companion.

And they slide out.

It's no good, Nat,' I tell him after they leave. 'Either the kid takes a dive or else the three of us ends up as risotto.'

Nat nods, and sighs very hard. Me, I reckon we are on to a fairly safe bet whether the kid understands what a dive is or not, especially when I hear Nat tell him to make sure and go down fighting genuine, because this introduces a couple of new words into the kid's midget vocabulary, and only confuses him further.

Next thing we know, a dame in a petal hat minces in with the news that they're waiting for us on court, and we trail after her for about three miles and eventually wind up in what looks like a dog pound. The only way to find out it wasn't a hard court championship would be to send off some of that brown weed for analysis, if you could scratch up enough to put in a matchbox. But there's a big crowd in the brokendown stand, and a distinguished one at that; I reckon most of Greek Street was there. Nat and me grab a ringside seat, and pray.

The first smell I get that things may be less straightforward than I thought is when the kid's opponent wins the toss and elects to serve into the sun and against the wind. At about the same moment, I notice that the umpire has sticking-plaster down both cheeks, leaving me with the uneasy feeling as to which side may have got to him first.

194

It didn't take long to find out. The kid's opponent serves four double faults and the kid naturally takes the first game to love. As they change over, a vice squeezes my neck; it is, of course, our new Sicilian partner, and I have a new worry in that I am going to spend the rest of my life with a perfect set of fingerprints around my throat, and when he twigs the risk of this, he may very well decide to destroy the evidence.

'Wossa goin on?' he hisses to Nat. 'Youra boy is cleanin up.'

'It's not his fault,' says Nat. 'There is clearly money involved in the kid's opponent, who is likewise attempting to dive.'

In the second game, the kid serves three double faults, which is fine, but at Love–40 he accidentally gets an ace. I close my eyes, and there is a very long silence, at the end of which an extremely shaky voice shrieks:

'NET!'

The hood next to me puts on a fat smile.

'We gotta to the net judge,' he murmurs. 'We tole him we breaka his finger if he doan play ball. No finger, no job, see?'

In the third game, with the kid's opponent serving, there's a sudden change of tactics: every time he throws up the ball, a ball-boy runs across the court, thereby allowing the server to pull a very authentic show of nerves and muff all his shots, to lose the game. It's then I notice the ball-boys is in fact all very short characters in long black overcoats and trilbies, and I realise these are not members of the Dr. Barnardo crowd. Fortunately, during the second change-over, a tall thin citizen with a violin case has a somewhat heated word with the ball-boys, after which they blow, very fast, and do not reappear.

At 89–88 in the first set, with the moon coming up and much of the crowd getting slightly restless and many needle games of five-card stud breaking out all over the auditorium, Nat and me are beginning to reckon the only solution is that this game is going on till about October at which point it will be abandoned due to snow, or something, which would at least be an honourable conclusion. Then things happen very fast. Nat's boy has just taken a glass of Lucozade at the break, comes out, serves four aces quicker than the eye can see, and before we have time to start a zig-zag run for the exit, the umpire screams:

'Game and first set to Snike, 90–88!'

At this, half the crowd gets very cheerful, and half gets very ugly, and at least two members of it grow very cold on account of any second we may suddenly get taken dead. However, all that happens is there's a commotion in the crowd and a pin-striped item is shoving his way through it with a Gladstone bag in one fist, and a stethoscope in his ears.

'Letta me through!' he shouts. 'I am a dockertor!'

He sprints on court, leans over Nat's kid, who has collapsed and is twitching about on the sideline, and runs back to grab the umpire's microphone.

'It issa my qualified medical opinion,' he announces, 'thatta some fink has gotta to the Lucozade onna behalf of the kid who issa full of dope, an' hereby dissaqualified! Game set anna match to the other guy, at 6 to 4!'

Naturally, pandemonium breaks out at this, but me and Nat manages to fight our way through to the kid, and rush him back to the dressing-room. I lean back against the door, very moist.

'Well, Nat,' I say, 'at least we save our skins. The kid is now out of the tournament, which means no more worries.'

Nat don't say nothing, just looks at me a bit funny. He puts on his coat, and turns to his boy, who is flat out on the couch.

'Get a lousy night's sleep, kid,' he says. 'It's a big day to-morrow and I want you should be nice and worn-out for the match.'

'Match?' I say. 'I don't get it.'

Nat's eyes roll over to me, very weary.

'You think *today* was bad,' he says. 'You ain't seen nothing yet.'

'How do you mean?' I ask.

'Tomorrow,' says Nat, 'he has to throw the doubles.'

Keeping Up With the
Puddle-ducks

'Hedgehogs, foxes, grey squirrels, and even woodmice are adapting their ways increasingly to suburban life in the London area, says a report compiled by the London Natural History Society.'

Daily Telegraph

Once upon a time there were four little Rabbits, and their names were Flopsy, Mopsy, Cotton-tail, and Peter. They lived with their Mother and Father in a sand-bank, underneath the root of a very big fir-tree.

All of which was fine until the Tiggy-Winkles moved into the root next door.

'Here,' said Mr. Rabbit, returning home from work one evening, 'there's a load of bleeding hedgehogs moved in at Number Three!'

The Rabbits scuttled to the window. Sure enough, there preening themselves in the evening sunlight of Wimbledon Common, was a family of hedgehogs. There was a mother hedgehog, and a father hedgehog, and seven little hedgehogs.

'I don't believe it!' cried Mrs. Rabbit. 'There's been Rabbits here as long as I can remember. My mother was here, and *her* mother, and *her* mother before that!'

'And that's only 1968,' said Mr. Rabbit, honking a sliver of frozen broccoli from the back of his throat. He examined it with tiny pink eyes, and wondered briefly why the human animals were growing vegetables in solid blocks, all of a sudden. A right old neighbourhood this turned out to be! A right old neighbourhood, and no mistake. You move in, clean your root up a bit, nice piece of regency-stripe fag-packet on the walls, trendy pink bog-paper beds, all the latest chicken wire windows, genuine champagne-glass to pee in, and what happens? You're not in ten minutes, before a cartload of bloody hedgehogs ups and cops the property next door. Lowering the whole tone of the neighbourhood. Bringing values down. Introducing their hedgehog ways all over the place.'

'I wouldn't care,' said Mrs. Rabbit, 'I mean I'm not prejudiced, I mean live and let live, I mean it takes all sorts, I mean there's good and bad in everyone. But they've got funny habits haven't they?'

'Breed like rabbits,' said her husband. 'I mean flies. Look, there's nine of 'em out there now. Be another half-dozen by Tuesday, or I'm no judge of hedgehog-flesh. Not to mention friends and relatives; soon as one hedgehog moves in, they're all in, 'n' they?' He pushed open the window with his nose. 'Here, you hedgehogs!' he shouted. 'Eff off!'

The Tiggy-Winkles smiled and nodded. Mr. Rabbit slammed the window shut, fuming.

'There you are!' he shouted. 'What did I tell you? Thick as two boards! Can't even speak bloody English. I mean, stands to reason. They got smaller brains than us rabbits. And talk about filthy habits! I could tell you a thing or two about hedgehogs.'

'What sort of habits, Dad?' said little Peter.

Mrs. Rabbit turned and fetched him a clout behind the left ear.

'You get back to your homework, you little creep!' she shrieked. 'Jemima Puddle-duck's Alfred can count up to six already, and he's only nine weeks old.'

'And he can swim,' said Mr. Rabbit gloomily. 'Bleeding prodigy. 'Why didn't we have a duck, mother?'

She glared at him.

'Sometimes I think you're as dumb as he is, Arnold,' she said bitterly. 'I don't know why I've put up with you all these years. I could've been somebody, improved my position in life, got somewhere. Instead of being stuck down here in a lousy root, with a bunch of rodents for neighbours.'

'That's right, blame me!' shouted Mr. Rabbit. 'Always going on about me not having no ambition, not getting on in the world, not being able to live up the Pond with the Puddle-ducks and Squirrel bloody Nutkin, when you haven't even got the basic bit of common sense necessary to lay an ordinary egg!' He turned back to his snivelling son. 'Fleas, lad, that's what filthy habits they got. All over 'em. Fleas. Not to mention the fact they eat worms.'

'There'll be the smell of worms all over the stairs,' moaned Mopsy.

'And parties all night,' muttered Mrs. Rabbit. 'You know what hedgehogs are like, always hanging about with gypsies.'

'Parties?' cried Flopsy, clapping her paws.

Her father wheeled on her savagely.

'I catch you going to them hedgehog parties across the road, I'll knock your ruddy block off!'

His wife glowered.

'God, you're common!' she said. 'Got a mouth like a stoat, you have. No wonder you never get anywhere. No wonder we're shunned by people of *ton*. I don't know what Mr. Jeremy Fisher will think when Cotton-tail brings him home, what with you yelling, and hedge-hogs smelling the place out, and everything.'

'Who?'

'Mr. Jeremy Fisher,' said Mrs. Rabbit, and a glow of pride riffled her peroxided fur. 'Cotton-tail's out with him now. A gentleman of impeccable family. A person of taste and distinction. With private income and own boat.'

'Very nice,' said Mr. Rabbit. 'I was thinking about retiring only this morning. Putting my feet up. Doing a bit of gardening, that kind of thing.'

'I shouldn't be surprised,' Mrs. Rabbit continued, 'if the Puddle-ducks don't start taking notice of us when they hear Cotton-tail's going steady with Mr. Jeremy Fisher.'

'He's not out of her class, is he?' murmured her husband. 'I shouldn't like to think of my daughter marrying above herself.'

'Where else is there to marry?' cried Mrs. Rabbit. 'Trouble with you, Rabbit, is you've got a yokel's mentality. This is Wimbledon, Rabbit, and if you want to get on here, you got to make something of yourself, get a status, mix with – '

The doorbell rang, hurling Mrs. Rabbit into a frenzy of dusting, straightening, smoothing down, kicking under chairs, arranging.

'It's him!' she cried. 'Mr. Jeremy Fisher bringing our Cotton-tail home. Oh, what a moment in a mother's life, Arnold, when her little girl brings home a gentleman of breeding what has his own riverside residence and a complete change of underwear for every day of the week!'

She flew, fluttering, to the door, and flung it wide.

Cotton-tail and Mr. Jeremy Fisher stood there.

And Mr. Rabbit looked at them.

And turned pale.

'He's a frog!' he gasped, finally. 'He's a ruddy frog!'

Mr. Jeremy Fisher, minuscule beside his vast fiancée, hopped elegantly into the room.

'Bonjour,' he said. 'What a spiffin' residence you 'ave here.'

Mrs. Rabbit, blushing as only rabbits can, curtsied cumbrously.

'Pleased to meet you, your worship,' she mumbled.

Mr. Jeremy Fisher demurred with an aristocratic glug.

'Ho my goodness!' he cried. 'There's no need to go running off at the mouth with titles and all that gear. I'm not a duke, ha-ha-ha, though I do 'ave a few bob stashed away, even if I do say it as shouldn't. Just think of me as one of the family.'

'Fat chance!' muttered Mr. Rabbit, watching his diminutive son-in-law-to-be shimmering some way beneath him in the setting sunlight. He turned abruptly, and followed his simpering wife into the kitchen.

'I trust you've a water-beetle or two in the larder,' he said, heavily. 'Or perhaps Mr. Jeremy Fisher would care to sink his upper-class choppers into a succulent newt pie? The sort of thing us rabbits keeps on hand, just in case our daughter comes home with something she's found in a drain and feels like marrying.'

'Shut up!' hissed Mrs. Rabbit. 'Just shut up! He's a gent, and he wants our Cotton-tail, and he's going to give her a chance to go up in the world, and you're not putting your spoke in, if you know what's good for you.'

'I know what's good for Cotton-tail,' retorted Mr. Rabbit, 'and that don't include a honeymoon with a frog.'

'All you think about is sex!' cried his wife. 'There's more to life than that. It's rumoured that Jeremy Fisher's riverside property contains a bath, cunningly fashioned from an old po.'

'It's also rumoured he sleeps in it,' said Mr. Rabbit. 'Which isn't surprising, considering he's a frog. I don't mind telling you, he's not exactly what I had in mind for a son-in-law.'

Mrs. Rabbit turned on him, eyes fiery pink.

'You're not fit to live in Wimbledon!' she screamed. 'You ought to be back in – aaaargh!'

'What is it?' cried Mr. Rabbit, as his wife staggered back, pointing at the window. He followed her finger. It was Jemima Puddle-duck, First Lady of the Common! And she was coming up their path. To their back door. Trembling, Mrs. Rabbit opened it.

'Good afternoon,' said Jemima Puddle-duck, 'I hope as how you'll pardon the intrusion, but I heard that my good friend Mr. Jeremy Fisher had called upon you, don't you know, and I thought I might just drop in and pass the time of day. Since we're all neighbours, what?'

Confused, ecstatic, palpitating, the Rabbits fell back, bowing.

'They're all in the parlour, your Grace, having a bit of a giggle,' croaked Mrs. Rabbit. 'Won't you go in, and me and Rabbit will be in in a couple of shakes, if that's all right.'

Jemima Puddle-duck waddled out. Mrs. Rabbit grabbed her husband to her. Together they stood, shaking.

'*See?*' she hissed. 'See what a bit of class in the person of a frog with his own business does for you? Rabbit, we are as good as up at Puddle-duck Hall, scoffing them petty fours and –'

She broke off suddenly. The Rabbits froze. From the front room, there issued a high and terrible ululation. It was a noise they knew. It was Cotton-tail. They pitter-pattered nervously through the little door.

Jemima Puddle-duck stood in the centre of the room. Watching her, noiseless and immobile, stood Mopsy, Flopsy, and Peter Rabbit. Only Cotton-tail howled.

'She's ate my fiancé!' she sobbed. 'She's ate Mr. Jeremy Fisher!'

Jemima Puddle-duck burped.

'Pardon *me*!' she said. 'What a crackin' good frog tea, Mrs. Rabbit. Absolutely top-hole! Well, must be toddlin' along.'

And she left. Broken, Mrs. Rabbit watched her disappear, silent.

'Just goes to show,' said Mr. Rabbit, at last, 'that being a frog's not all it's cracked up to be.'

But nobody was listening to him.

How Odd of God!

'Cannon to right of them, Nigel!'

'Cannon to left of them, Freddie!'

'Cannon in front of them ...'

' ... volley'd and somethinged! I know, old man.'

'Staggering!'

'Inspiring!'

'Stirring! Was there a heart-cockle unwarmed, old man?'

'Or a single untrembling lip?'

'The short hairs, old chap. Stood on end. Like quills upon the something eglantine. When they rode out across the burning sands, wheeling here, jabbing there, here a push, there a thrust ...'

'Everywhere a blitzkrieg.'

'The panache, Nigel! The devil-may-care! Joy in the morning, sun on steel, the reek of the cordite!'

'But backs to the wall, old man.'

'True. Bite on the bullet.'

'Fight on the beaches.'

'Quite. An hour to play and the last man in.'

'Like Horatio.'

'Like Agincourt.'

'Like Flores.'

'In the Azores?'

'That's the one, old man. Like Sir Francis.'

'Which one, old chap?'

'Both, old man. Like Rorke's Drift.'

'Khartoum.'

'Kohima.'

'*Ils ne passeront pas,* Nigel!'

'But more – more *British*, Freddie.'

'The very word, old man. September 1940.'

'Exact parallel. You've a firm grasp of history's myriad patterns, Freddie.'

'One tries to keep up, old man.'

'Brave, beardless lads, plucked from the squash courts, hurled against the snarling foe, madly outnumbered, their flimsy machines the last ditch before the very annihilation of all that civilisation means.'

'Thin red line, Nigel.'

'Scramble!'

'Contact!'

'While all the world wondered!'

'Plucky little Jews!'

'Israelis, Freddie.'

'I'm sorry?'

'Israelis, old man, Plucky little Israelis.'

'Ah. Quite. One can't really think of them as Jews, can one?'

'Impossible. Not when one knows all the facts about Jews oneself. I mean, after all, it would have been utterly beyond Jews to have defeated the Arabs, wouldn't it?'

'Entirely. They wouldn't have fought, for a start.'

'Not their style at all. They'd have probably formed a cartel and made a below-market bid for the Gaza Strip.'

'Having first bought out the U.N. Emergency Force for a pittance.'

'And gone on to build cheap jerry-built houses. They'd have made a takeover bid for the Sinai Peninsula, too. Turned it into a vast gown factory.'

'Filling the world with cheap shoddy pyjamas.'

'And inflammable nightdresses.'

'Undermining Christian morality with overpriced miniskirts.'

'Which brings up the whole question of Jerusalem, Freddie. The Israelis went out of their way to avoid damaging the holy places, whereas . . . '

' . . . the Jews would have taken advantage of this to exercise their well-known desire for revenge on Christians. They'd have bought the Holy Sepulchre . . . '

' . . . with money subscribed by International Financiers

who'd screwed it out of widows and orphans . . . '

' . . . razed it to the ground, and put up a kosher restaurant.'

'You know they slaughter cows by holding them up by the tail until their eyes drop out?'

'I thought that was guinea-pigs, old man.'

'They probably *started* on guinea-pigs, old chap.'

'And worked up. That would be their way, wouldn't it?'

'Oh, they're ambitious, all right. I wouldn't deny them that.'

'Nor I. My wife knows one, and she said . . . '

'I say, they're not moving in round your way, are they?'

'Good God, no! No, she met this one at the theatre. There was a mix-up over the seats, and they had to swop round.'

'Ah. And was he ambitious?'

'Incredibly. That was the definite impression she got. Incredibly ambitious. And probably avaricious, too.'

'They'd pawn their own grandmothers, most of them.'

'Which is hardly the sort of thing one could imagine Israelis doing. Not fighter pilots.'

'Not tank commanders.'

'Not much time to pawn your grandmother during a lightning pincer movement, is there?'

'Quite. Which more or less proves what we were saying.'

'Not of course, that one can *automatically* identify a Jew by his readiness to put the family in hock.'

'No. I think we can claim to be a little more sophisticated in our judgment that that, old man.'

'Quite. I think we're capable of looking all round a question, Nigel.'

'Certainly. Capable of seeing further than our own noses.'

'Not like some people, ha-ha-ha!'

'I say, that's rather good, Freddie. Did you just make that up, old chap?'

'Came to me in a flash, old man.'

'Wish I'd thought of it. Wonderful thing, a sense of humour.'

'True. Helps enormously. There's a serious point there, mind.'

'Not with you, old man.'

'The old physical characteristsics, Nigel. Think back over the newsreels. I assume you've been following the war on the box?'

'Glued to it, Freddie. Jolly good thing the Test Match started the day the war went flat, actually. Would have been a hell of a let-down otherwise, wouldn't it?'

'Absolute wasteland, old man. Pity it wasn't the Aussies, actually. Don't want to follow a thing like a good rousing shoot-'em-up war with a Second XI fixture like the Indians. Still, better than nothing. No, what I was getting at was the remarkable shortage of hooked noses in the Israeli army.'

'Good Lord. I hadn't even thought to look! But now you mention it . . . there wasn't much in the way of cringing, shuffling physiques, either, was there? Or that hangdog expression one's read so much about.'

'Only goes to prove our point, doesn't it? And how many of them did you notice talking with their hands?'

'Can't remember a single gesture, old chap. Mind you, they *were* holding guns and things, which makes the old hand-waving a bit tricky.'

'Oh, I wouldn't say that. You can always park the Sten in one hand while you gesticulate with the other, if you really want to. It's what the Jews would have done, if they'd been there.'

'Except that they wouldn't be holding a Sten in the first place. Unless they happened to be selling it to somebody.'

'And that's another thing, Nigel. There was precious little haggling that I could see.'

'None at all. In fact, Israel quite pointedly refused to bargain, so there you are.'

'Case proven, old man. Q.E.D.'

'Glad we got that settled. Any plans for the weekend, Freddie?'

'Nothing specific. Thought I might play a round or two of golf.'

'Might join you. I say, that reminds me – did you see there was a move in some circles to waive the club's restrictions against the old Chosen People?'

206

'Heard a rumour, old man. Won't come to anything, though. Bloody preposterous. People don't realise what they're like. Don't realise what harm they can do to a golf club. They absolutely refuse to mix. It's one of their most notorious characteristics. They exclude other people entirely. That's why we've got to keep them out, Nigel.'

'Absolutely with you, Freddie. One hundred per cent. Of course, if an Israeli were to apply . . .'

'. . . we might just consider it, mightn't we?'

'Oh, yes. Always provided he was the right sort of chap.'

ALSO AVAILABLE IN CORONET

ALAN COREN

☐ 20998 4	Golfing for Cats	60p
☐ 21477 5	The Sanity Inspector (large format)	70p
☐ 19912 1	The Sanity Inspector	60p
☐ 22299 9	The Dog It Was That Died	80p

DIRK GIRLING ETC

☐ 20145 2	Would You Believe This Too?	60p
☐ 22007 4	Would You Believe It, Doctor?	75p

ed. WILLIAM DAVIS

☐ 20999 2	The Punch Book of Health	80p

JOHNNY HART

☐ 18820 0	B.C. On The Rocks	50p
☐ 20653 5	B.C. One More Time	50p
☐ 16880 3	B.C. Big Wheel	50p

All these books are available at your local bookshop or newsagent, or can be ordered direct from the publisher. Just tick the titles you want and fill in the form below.

Prices and availability subject to change without notice.

CORONET BOOKS, P.O. Box 11, Falmouth, Cornwall.

Please send cheque or postal order, and allow the following for postage and packing:

U.K. – One book 22p plus 10p per copy for each additional book ordered, up to a maximum of 82p.

B.F.P.O. and EIRE – 22p for the first book plus 10p per copy for the next 6 books, thereafter 4p per book.

OTHER OVERSEAS CUSTOMERS – 30p for the first book and 10p per copy for each additional book.

Name ....

Address ....

....